VISUAL QUICKSTART GUIDE

AppleWorks 5

FOR WINDOWS AND MACINTOSH

C. Ann Brown

 Peachpit Press

Visual QuickStart Guide
AppleWorks 5 for Windows and Macintosh
C. Ann Brown

Peachpit Press

1249 Eighth Street
Berkeley, CA 94710
(800) 283-9444
(510) 524-2178
(510) 524-2221 (fax)

Find us on the World Wide Web at: http://www.peachpit.com

Peachpit Press is a division of Addison Wesley Longman

Editor: Corbin Collins
Production Coordinators: Mimi Heft, Lisa Brazieal
Compositor: David Van Ness
Cover design: The Visual Group

ISBN: 0-201-35403-9

0 9 8 7 6 5 4 3 2 1

Printed and bound in the United States of America

Printed on recycled paper

Dedication:

This book is dedicated to Corbin Collins, the most patient book editor anyone could find; to Dr. Yun Chen and Dr. Yu Xie who made it possible for me to work at all; and to David Ralph Butler for waiting 16 or 34 years, depending on who is counting; to my aunts Lucille Smalley of Santa Rosa and Tommeye Gene Welch of Santa Rosa and San Antonio for always being there when I needed them.

About the Author:

Dr. C. Ann Brown is a long time computer user, aficionado of the Internet, and researcher for Sentius Corporation in Palo Alto, California. She is the author of *FileMaker Pro For Macintosh: Visual QuickStart Guide* and *ClarisWorks 4 For Macintosh: Visual QuickStart Guide*, both for Peachpit Press. She has daily conversations with her numerous parrots, friends, and students—mostly on the Internet. When not writing, she can be found cleaning parrot cages.

TABLE OF CONTENTS

GETTING STARTED

Figure 1.1 AppleWorks contains all of the tools needed to successfully run a small business, write a great school paper, or surf the Internet.

What is AppleWorks?

AppleWorks has definitely grown up and now possesses more capabilities than most expensive office suites or programs currently available.

AppleWorks is designed so that it is exceedingly easy to use, that the steps to accomplish the tasks are clear, and that the program features all of the things you might want to do—from simple word processing to performing a mail merge, or even connecting with the Internet.

This book gives step-by-step instructions for both Macintosh and Windows 95 users to get you started and features complete screen shots so you know you are looking at the correct menu or dialog box.

We want to make the venture into AppleWorks as easy as possible.

So let's go to work with AppleWorks…

Program modes

AppleWorks is an integrated program—that means AppleWorks is really six programs in one program. Each of these programs functions both alone and with the other program modules, allowing easy use of information from one module in another module. For instance, it is easy to use information from the spreadsheet mode inside of the word processing module.

Word Processing

for writing letters and reports, performing mail merge for sending a single letter to multiple recipients

Spreadsheets

for solving financial questions, keeping track of numbers and information, making summaries of that information, then graphing it.

Database

for storing names and addresses, inventories, student's grade, and any other type of repetitive information

Drawing

for designing graphics, newsletters with boxes and art, and for rendering architectural drawings

Painting

for freehand drawing and design using color and bit-mapped drawing techniques

Communications

for accessing the Internet service provider, dialing local bulletin board services, and dialing out to other computers such as service bureaus.

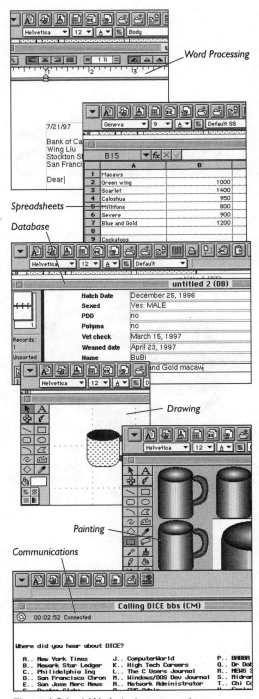

Figure 1.2 AppleWorks is six programs in one.

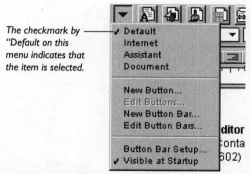

The checkmark by "Default on this menu indicates that the item is selected.

Figure 1.3 Available toolbars are listed on the left side of the Default toolbar. Use additional toolbars by selecting them from this list.

File	Edit	Format	Font
New...			⌘N
Open...			⌘O
Insert...			
Close			⌘W
Save			⌘S
Save As...			⇧⌘S
Revert			
Document Summary...			
Library			▶
Macros			▶
Mail Merge...			
Page Setup...			
Print...			⌘P
Quit			⌘Q

Figure 1.4 The Document Summary menu choice on the File Menu sets passwords for documents.

What's new in AppleWorks?

AppleWorks is simply astounding. The program is now richer, but is still just as easy as it was in previous versions. In this version you will find:

Toolbars

Fully customizable toolbars. You can create your own toolbar, rearrange buttons on a toolbar, or place a macro on a tool bar (see Figure 1.3).

Macros

Macros can be recorded in any of the AppleWorks modules and then played back in any of the other modules. This means you can create a macro in word processing, and use that same macro in the spreadsheet module.

Internet access

Access the Internet from within AppleWorks— Dial any Internet Service Provider or local BBS (bulletin board service).

Style sheets

Use style sheets in all modules to make work look more professional.

Flexible frames

Import spreadsheets into word processing, create frames in drawing and import text frames, graphics, and spreadsheet frames.

Password protection

Protect all AppleWorks files with a password or assign passwords to each file individually (see Figure 1.4).

For Macintosh users

This section is for Macintosh users, if you are a Windows 95 user, turn to "Starting AppleWorks" on page 10.

If you have just purchased a Macintosh, you probably have AppleWorks already installed on it. The next section helps familiarize you with basic Macintosh operations.

If you are an experienced Macintosh user, skip ahead in this chapter to "Getting Around in AppleWorks" on page 12 for more information.

Starting the Macintosh

Fortunately starting the Macintosh is easy. All you need to do is push the start or power button on the keyboard. The power key has a triangle that faces left on it. This key is usually located at the top or the right side of the keyboard.

It may take the computer a few seconds to start all of the programs it needs to run smoothly. Eventually you'll see the main Menu bar (see Figure 1.5).

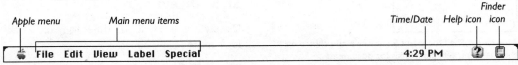

Figure 1.5 The main Menu bar on a Macintosh.

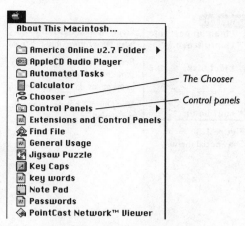

The Chooser

Control panels

Figure 1.6 The Apple Menu

Figure 1.7 The View menu.

Apple menu

The Apple menu lists all of the useful Apple controls. Each Macintosh is set up a little differently. One item, the Chooser, is how you select a printer to use to print files. Control panels allow you to modify sound, date and time displays, and background or desktop displays (see Figure 1.6).

File menu

The File menu lets you set up a new file folder, print the desktop, or get information about a program in order to increase memory for that program.

Edit menu

The Edit menu lets you cut, copy or paste items on the desktop. You can also view the clipboard, which contains the last item that was copied.

View menu

View lets you change the way icons may be seen in menus (see Figure 1.7). You have a choice of seeing the file names by:

■ Small icon

■ Icon (large icon)

■ Name (alphabetical)

■ Size (smallest to largest)

■ Kind (application type)

■ Date (most recent to oldest)

Label menu

The Label menu on the main Apple menu bar adds color to objects and icons.

FOR MACINTOSH USERS

Special menu

You can use the Special menu to erase a floppy disk or hard disk. (Be careful not to erase your main hard disk!) You also use this menu to empty the Trash (see Figure 1.8).

To erase a disk:

1. Click the desktop icon that represents the floppy disk to be erased.

2. Select Erase from the Special menu. The confirmation dialog box appears.

3. Click the OK button to confirm that you want to erase the disk.

   or

   Click the Cancel button if the disk is not supposed to be erased.

To delete files:

1. Click the file you want to delete.

2. Drag the file on top of the trash icon. The icon will turn dark when the file is dragged into proper position.

3. Select Empty Trash from the Special menu. The confirmation dialog box appears.

4. Click the OK button if you really want to erase the files

   or

   If you do not want to erase files click the cancel button.

✔ Tip

- To restore or recover files from the Trash double-click the trash icon and drag the files out of the trash and into their proper folders.

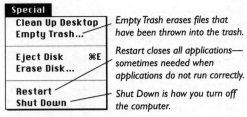

Figure 1.8
The Special menu.

Empty Trash erases files that have been thrown into the trash.

Restart closes all applications—sometimes needed when applications do not run correctly.

Shut Down is how you turn off the computer.

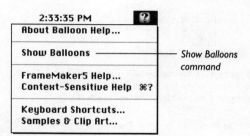

Figure 1.9 Help on the Apple main menu

Show Balloons command

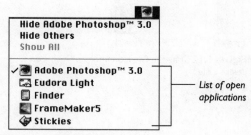

Figure 1.10 Application menu

List of open applications

Balloon Help menu

Balloon help, located on the help menu, gives you automatic pop up balloons. These balloons appear on the desktop, or on menu bars and other locations in application programs (see Figure 1.9).

To turn on Balloon help:

1. Move the pointer on top of the Help menu and hold the mouse button down.

2. Let go of the mouse button when you are on top of the Show Balloons menu choice.

Application menu

The Application menu is located on the far right side of the main menu bar. This menu lists all of the applications that are currently running. The current program in use appears on this pop up menu with a checkmark beside it (see Figure 1.10).

To use the Application menu:

1. Move the pointer to the icon at the top right of the screen and hold down the mouse button.

2. Drag the cursor down to any program you want to use. The program you choose should appear in a highlighted bar.

3. Let go of the mouse button. The program appears.

FOR MACINTOSH USERS

Icons

To look at the contents of any disk double-click the disk icon.

Hard disk icons

Hard disks contain programs and document files. Be careful never to erase a hard disk or all of the programs could be erased.

Floppy disk icons

Floppy disks are the portable 3½ inch disks used with the Macintosh and the PC. Macintosh machines will also read 3½ inch disks intended for use with the PC (see Figure 1.11).

Once the Macintosh is started if you place an uninitialized floppy disk into the floppy disk drive, the computer then tries to initialize the disk. Initializing disks is the computer's way of getting a disk ready to receive data. Initialize also erases any old information that was on a disk.

Zip disks look similar to 3½ inch floppies, but they're thicker and wider. Zip disks won't fit into floppy disk drives on either Macintosh or Windows 95 computers. (You need a Zip drive to use Zip disks.)

The Trash icon

The Trash icon is the place to put files to be erased (see Figure 1.12).

To erase files from a disk:

- Drag them into the trash.

- Select Erase Files from the Special menu. The file is erased.

AppleWorks Book

Figure 1.11 This floppy disk is a PC disk. Although you can read many—but not all—PC files, you can't run PC programs on the Macintosh automatically.

The Trash icon   Time to empty the trash.

Trash   Trash

Figure 1.12 Drag the File icon into the Trash icon to delete a file.

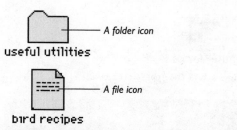

useful utilities

— A folder icon

bird recipes

— A file icon

Figure 1.13 File folders look like manila folders. You move files into a folder by dragging them on top of the folder.

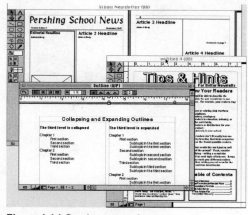

Figure 1.14 Overlapping windows.

File and Folder icons

File icons are often shown as smaller versions of a logo or startup file icon. They also appear as a page of paper with typing on it.

Folders appear looking just like manila folders (see Figure 1.13). Folders can contain files, programs, or other folders. Folders are the principal management tool for both the Macintosh and Windows systems. Folders are called directories sometimes on Windows or DOS machines.

Window

A window is a rectangular area with borders that can contain files or programs. You can have more than one window open at a time, and windows often overlap, or lay on top of each other (see Figure 1.14).

Windows contain scroll bars so you can see contents that are temporarily out of view in other portions of the window.

Starting AppleWorks

Starting AppleWorks on a Macintosh

Double-click the AppleWorks icon or double-click any file that was previously created in AppleWorks. See Figure 1.15.

Starting AppleWorks in Windows 95

You may start AppleWorks from the desktop icon or the Start menu.

To start from the desktop double-click the AppleWorks icon.

To open AppleWorks from the Start menu:

1. Click the Start button on the bottom taskbar of Windows 95.

2. Click the Programs choice on the start menu. The Programs submenu appears.

3. Click the AppleWorks choice on the Programs submenu. The AppleWorks icon appears on the submenu.

4. Click the AppleWorks icon. AppleWorks starts.

AppleWorks

Figure 1.15 The AppleWorks icon.

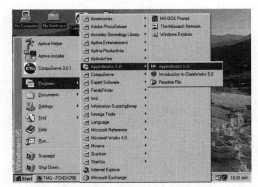

Figure 1.16 The Start menu for one computer using Windows 95.

Table 1.1

Macintosh and Windows key equivalents		
MACINTOSH KEY	WINDOWS KEY	USES
Command [⌘]	Ctrl [Control]	Commands on menus
Control	Alt	Commands on menus
Delete	Backspace	Deletes text backward
Return	Enter or return	Ends a paragraph or enters typed information
Clear	Delete	Deletes highlighted information from the file

 Trash
 Recycle Bin

Figure 1.17 The Macintosh Trash is equivalent to the Windows 95 Recycle Bin.

Macintosh and Windows key equivalents

Some commands are slightly different on Windows 95 than they are on the Macintosh. Although this is a cross-platform book, it is handy to know how to "translate" commands from Macintosh to Windows. We will tell you what the appropriate Windows command is as well as what the Macintosh command is throughout the book.

Moving files around is roughly the same on the Macintosh as it is in Windows, and deleting files is only slightly different. To delete files on the Macintosh, drag files into the trash icon. In Windows 95, drag files into the recycling bin (see Figure 1.17).

As various issues appear regarding running AppleWorks for Windows, this book shows you both Macintosh and Windows commands. Use Table 1.1 on this page to help you get started.

Getting around in AppleWorks

AppleWorks contains pull-down and pop up menus, shortcut keys, and toolbars with buttons like many other popular programs. Functions available from menus, buttons and shortcuts are greatly expanded in this version of AppleWorks.

Opening screen

Double-clicking the AppleWorks program icon causes the opening screen to appear (see Figure 1.18). This screen gives you the choice of word processing, drawing, painting, spreadsheets, database, or communications modules.

You also have the choice of starting with template files that are shipped with AppleWorks. These template files are called Assistants or Stationery. Assistants help save time by creating a file that is partially completed.

Each time a new project is started in AppleWorks the opening menu appears and you must choose Create New Document or Use Assistant or Stationery.

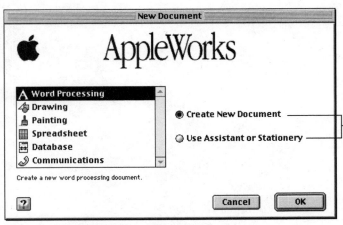

Click the "New Document" or "Use Assistant or Stationary" radio buttons to choose whether you want to start with a blank piece of paper or a pre-formatted document.

Figure 1.18 The AppleWorks opening screen.

Main menu bar with the File menu selected.

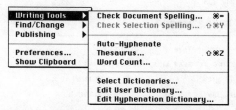

Figure 1.19 Menus in AppleWorks

Keyboard shortcuts on the right-hand side of the commands are a quicker way to perform a task. The ⌘ key is the Command key on the Macintosh keyboard.

Small triangles on the menu indicate a sub-menu appears when that menu item is selected.

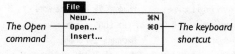

Figure 1.20 Submenu of the Writing Tools menu choice on the Edit menu in AppleWorks Word Processing.

The Open command

The keyboard shortcut

Figure 1.21 The top of the File menu showing the Open command, with the keyboard shortcut for opening a file appearing on the right side of the menu.

Here's an enlargement of the Open file button on the main toolbar.

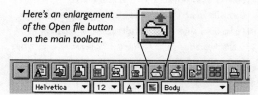

Figure 1.22 The main toolbar of the word processing module in AppleWorks. The Open file button opens a previously saved file.

Navigating AppleWorks

AppleWorks is navigated by using menus, toolbars, and buttons.

Menus

Menus are the backbone of all programs. Although many actions can be found on buttons and toolbars, menus often contain additional functions, or allow exploring a function in greater depth.

Menus contain commands and keyboard shortcuts. Some menu items have a sub-menu attached (see Figures 1.19 and 1.20). Keyboard shortcuts are shown on the right-hand side of the menu.

Toolbars

Toolbars are one of the most basic ways to access commands in AppleWorks. Toolbars are form of shortcut. Instead of using menus or keyboard shortcuts, you can simply click a button to perform a task.

Click any button on the toolbar to use the toolbar shortcut, such as the Open button on the main toolbar to open a previously saved file. Commands on the toolbar are also available on pull-down menus (see Figures 1.21 and 1.22).

In AppleWorks you can also create your own toolbar made up of macros or the collection of toolbar buttons that AppleWorks includes in this software package.

NAVIGATING APPLEWORKS

Keyboard shortcuts

The File menu in AppleWorks is a good example of a menu that shows both commands and shortcuts. Most shortcut keys are the same in all programs on both the Macintosh and on Windows 95. Use Table 1.1 on page 11 and Table 1.2 at right for a list of common shortcut keys.

When using shortcut keys, don't push two or three keys down simultaneously. First hold down the Command key, then hold down the Shift key if you need it. While you are still holding down those keys, quickly tap the appropriate letter of the alphabet. Then let go of the keys.

Moving around

You can move around inside of a AppleWorks document, or any Macintosh or Windows 95 document using any one of three methods:

- Click near text to be edited or inserted, or click a picture to be moved or deleted.

- Click the scroll bars that appear on the right side and horizontally across the bottom of the window. Scroll bars move in larger increments if you click either side of the scroll box.

- If you have an extended keyboard that features keys such as "home," "page up" or "page down" move by using those keys.

Table 1.3 is a chart with common key combinations for moving around for the Macintosh and Windows 95.

Table 1.2

Shortcut Keys for Macintosh and Windows 95		
MACINTOSH	WINDOWS 95	USED FOR
⌘-S	Control+S	Save a file
⌘-P	Control+P	Print a file
⌘-Q	Control+Q	Quit the program
⌘-C	Control+C	Copy highlighted text
⌘-X	Control+X	Cut highlighted text
⌘-V	Control+V	Paste text or graphics
⌘-Z	Control+Z	Undo the most recent action
⌘-A	Control+A	Select everything in a file
⌘-. (period)	Control+Break	Cancel a command such as printing, or quit a dialog box

Table 1.3

Moving around	
KEY COMBINATION	USED FOR
MOVING BETWEEN LINES OR CHARACTERS	
Right arrow	right one character
Left arrow	left one character
Up arrow	Up one line
Down arrow	down one line
MOVING BETWEEN WORDS	
Option-right arrow	Macintosh: Right one word
Control+right arrow	Windows 95: Right one word
MOVING FROM ONE END OF THE LINE TO THE OTHER	
⌘-right arrow	Macintosh: end of line
⌘-left arrow	Macintosh: beginning of line
End	Windows 95: end of line
Home	Windows 95: beginning of line
MOVING FROM PARAGRAPH TO PARAGRAPH	
Option-Up arrow	Macintosh: beginning of paragraph
Option-Down arrow	Macintosh: end of paragraph
Control+Up arrow	Windows 95: beginning of paragraph
Control+Down arrow	Windows 95: end of paragraph

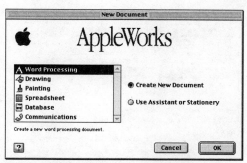

Figure 1.23 Each time a new document is opened from the File menu, you see the menu with the six modules of AppleWorks. You may switch freely between modules at any time.

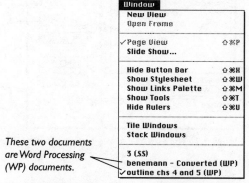

These two documents are Word Processing (WP) documents.

Figure 1.24 Documents that are currently open are listed on the bottom of the Window menu. An abbreviation in parentheses after the document indicates which module was used to create the document.

Switching between modes

AppleWorks has six different modules: word processing, spreadsheets, database, drawing, painting and communications (see Figure 1.23).

To switch between parts of AppleWorks and start a new document in a different module:

- Choose New from the File menu, or press ⌘-N on the Macintosh or Control+N on Windows 95. The opening screen appears.

  or

- Choose Open from the File menu, or press ⌘-O on the Macintosh, or Control+O on Windows 95. This opens another document in any of the AppleWorks modules.

The View menu also lists all documents that are currently open (see Figure 1.24). You may open as many documents in any module as the computer allows you. The number of documents that can be opened at one time depends upon how much RAM the computer has.

Switching between open documents

Select the document to be used from the View menu. If you want to open a Word Processing document from the View menu while you are working in Communications, for example, AppleWorks automatically starts up the Word Processing module for you.

Saving a document

When a document is finished in any module, remember to save it. Saving a document records it on the disk.

To save a document:

1. Choose Save from the File menu (press ⌘-S on the Macintosh, Control+S on Windows 95). The Save As Dialog box appears (see Figure 1.25 and 1.26).

   This dialog box shows you where the file is placed, and lets you choose a new file folder or new drive for the file if you want to change the location of the file.

2. If you want to save in the default location, or the location indicated in the Save dialog box, type a name in the document name box.

3. Click the Save button. The document is saved.

The Save As... Dialog box

Use Save As... to change either the name or the location of a document.

To save a file to a new location instead of the default location:

1. Move mouse pointer to the top pop up menu (A) and hold the mouse button down.

2. Navigate to the folder where you want to save the file. If you want to save the file on the desktop, click the desktop button (B).

3. Type a name in the Filename box (C).

4. Click the Save button when you are finished.

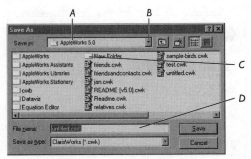

Figure 1.25 The Save As... dialog box in Windows 95.

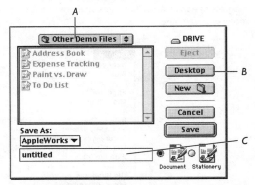

Figure 1.26 The Save As... dialog box on a Macintosh.

Type the keywords for the Help
topic you need in the keyword box

Windows
close box

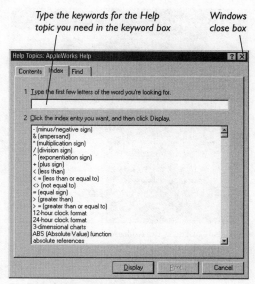

Figure 1.27 Windows 95 Help index.

AppleWorks Help

Help shows brief descriptions and simple steps to accomplish actions in AppleWorks.

To use Help:

1. Mac users press the Help key or press ⌘-?. Windows 95 users press the F1 key. The Help dialog box appears.

2. Click the Index tab at the top of the Help box. The Index dialog box appears (see Figure 1.27). The Help index is an alphabetical categorization of help topics.

3. Scroll down through the index list until reaching the desired help topic.

   or

   Type the first few letters of the help topic (for example, type "pri" for print). Help automatically moves to topics that start with those letters.

4. Click the topic when the appropriate topic appears.

5. Click the Go to Topic button (Macintosh users) or the Display button (Windows 95 users). The help box appears.

Printing AppleWorks help

■ Click the Print button at the bottom of the Help dialog box to print a Help topic.

Closing help

■ Click the close box in the help dialog box.

   If the help icon is still active or open, use the application icon to switch back to AppleWorks. Help always closes when AppleWorks closes.

APPLEWORKS HELP

Assistants and Stationery

AppleWorks assistants and stationery are more beautiful and more complete than ever. The difference between an assistant and stationery is that assistants have some automation built in. This automation helps fill in the blanks or other necessary elements.

Check out "Address List Assistant" (see Figure 1.28) for an example of an automated Assistant.

To use assistants or stationery:

1. Press ⌘-N on the Macintosh, or Control+N on Windows 95 to start a new file.

2. Select the Assistants or the stationery radio button. The New Document dialog box appears with a list of stationery and Assistants templates.

3. Click the desired assistant or stationery.

If you choose an automated assistant, buttons appear in the dialog box that give instructions on what to do to complete the assistant. The buttons below are from the Certificates assistant. Notice the button on the right that says "Next." To continue on to the next screen in the Assistants menu, click the Next button.

✔ Tip

■ Use Assistants to help make documents quickly. Assistants all contain automation, while stationery files are just blank template documents.

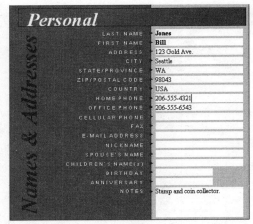

Figure 1.28 This is the Address stationery from the Database module of AppleWorks.

BEGINNING
WORD PROCESSING

Starting out

Word processing is the most commonly used form of computing. From simple letters to our friends, to more complicated newsletters and mail merges, word processing can be a basic exercise or something more complicated.

Creating a document

Start creating a word processing document by following these steps:

1. Start the AppleWorks program by double-clicking the AppleWorks icon. The New Document dialog box appears (see Figure 2.1).

2. Click Word Processing in the program list of the New Document dialog box.

3. Click the OK button.

   or

   Double-click Word Processing in the program list of the New Document dialog box.

✔ Tips

■ Instead of selecting a program module or a file, then clicking the OK button, you may always use a double-click to start a program or open a file. When you double-click, the second click is like clicking on the OK button (see Figure 2.2).

■ You can also start a new document by pressing ⌘-N on the Macintosh or Control+N on Windows 95.

■ If you do not see the file in the Open Dialog box and not want to translate a file, click the Document Type drop down menu and select the file type. The file then appears in the Open dialog box document list.

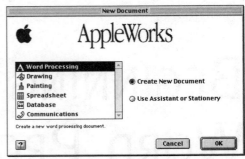

Figure 2.1 The New Document dialog box.

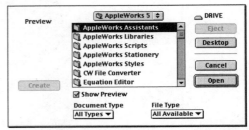

Figure 2.2 Double-click a file name in the Open dialog box to open a file more quickly.

Zoom percentage
Zoom-out
Zoom-in   Page indicator

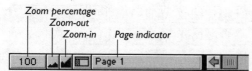

Figure 2.3 The Zoom bar is located on the lower left side of the word processing window.

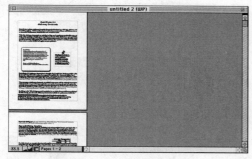

Figure 2.4 This document is zoomed out so that the document shows at 33% of its normal size. This was accomplished by clicking the decrease size button on the zoom bar three times.

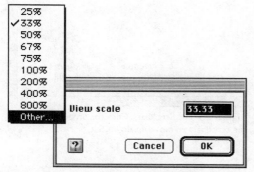

Figure 2.5 You may choose a view size from the pop up menu (left) or type a size in the size box of the View Scale dialog box (right).

Getting a better view

Zooming in on work to see a detail or zooming out to see how the general layout works is accomplished by using the zoom bar at the bottom of the word processing window. Although the document may appear smaller or bigger on the screen, the document still prints at normal size (see Figure 2.3).

To decrease size:

- Click the Zoom-out button on the lower left side of the word processing window.

  If you click the decrease size button more than once, each time the document in the window will appear smaller (see Figure 2.4).

To increase size:

- Click the Zoom-in button on the lower left side of the word processing window.

  You may also click the increase size button more than once.

To change the view:

You can change the view from one of the preset views by using the size indicator button.

1. Click the size indictor button. A size selection choice pops up (see Figure 2.5).

2. Pick a size from this list or click the Other... menu choice. When you click the Other... menu choice, the View Scale dialog box appears.

3. Type the size at which you want to view the document in the size box.

4. Click the OK button when you are done.

Shortcuts

Shortcuts include a variety of buttons and icons that can be used to invoke commands faster or easier than they can be invoked when using menus.

Shortcuts can be found on the:

Button Bar—contains buttons that are commands, such as Print or Save (see Figure 2.6).

Document title bar—resizes the document window, closes the application, or shows the name of the current document (see Figure 2.7).

Ruler bar—sets tabs, resets margins or indents a paragraph (see Figure 2.8).

Scrollbars—move up or down the page or from left to right in small or large increments (see Figure 2.9).

- Click the button on the scrollbar that contains an arrow to move in small increments.

- Click the arrow that points up on the vertical scrollbar to move up in the document.

- Click the arrow that points down to move down in the document.

- Click the arrow that points to the right to see the right side of the document.

- Click the arrow that points to the left to see the left side of the document.

Figure 2.6 Each button on the Button Bar performs a function that is also on a menu.

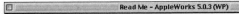

Figure 2.7 The Title bar tells you which program you are using and gives the name of the document.

Figure 2.8 The Ruler bar. The triangles on each end of the ruler bar represent the left and right indents.

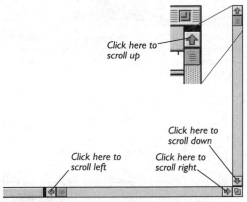

Click here to scroll up

Click here to scroll down

Click here to scroll left

Click here to scroll right

Figure 2.9 The Scrollbars. Click the arrow buttons on the scrollbars to move up, down, left, or right.

The word processing screen

The screen display in each program module of AppleWorks looks slightly different. Here are the main parts of the word processing screen (see Figure 2.10).

Margins and column dividers appear as light gray dotted lines. You cannot type outside of the margins.

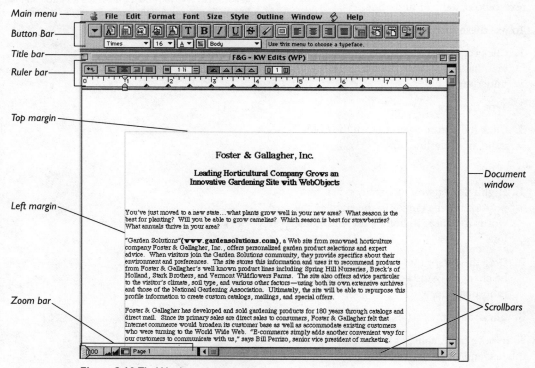

Figure 2.10 The Word processing screen.

The Button Bar

The Button Bar contains buttons for commands that may also be found on the menus (see Figure 2.11). If you have turned on Balloon Help, move the mouse pointer on top of any button. Balloon help then shows the function of that button performs. To use the button, just click once.

Some buttons change text. For example, the bold, italic, and underline buttons change text to bold, italic or underline.

To use these formatting buttons:

1. Click the button just before typing the text that is to appear in bold, italic, or underline.

2. Type the text.

3. Click the button again to turn the bold, italic, or underline off.

or

1. Highlight text you've already typed by positioning the cursor to the right of the words to appear in bold, italic, or underline.

2. Drag the cursor over the words that are to be changed while holding down the mouse button.

3. Click the appropriate button.

To remove bold, italic, or underline, highlight the text and click the bold, italic or underline button.

Figure 2.11 The Main menu contains many commands that are also on the Button bar. You may use shortcut keys such as ⌘-B for Bold, or press the B button on the Button bar, or access Bold by clicking the Style menu and selecting Bold.

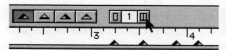

Figure 2.12 This pointer is in perfect position to change the number of columns. Notice how the tip of the pointer is on the button.

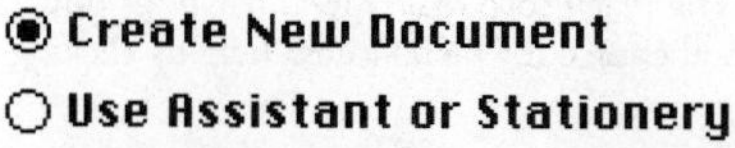

Figure 2.13 Radio buttons are active when the center of the button is dark.

Figure 2.14 These push buttons change a paragraph alignment from left, to center, right, or full justification. The darker button on the left is chosen.

| Helvetica ▼ | 12 ▼ | A ▼ | Body ▼ |

Figure 2.15 Pop up list buttons.

Using buttons

To use a button, make sure the tip of the pointer touches the button icon.

When the cursor is on top of a button, click the mouse to activate the button (see Figure 2.12).

There are three basic types of buttons in AppleWorks.

Radio buttons

Choose a radio button by clicking in the circle by the button. When the center of the circle is dark, the radio button is chosen (see Figure 2.13).

Push buttons

Normally square or lozenge shaped, push buttons are the most common button in any program. Examples include the justification buttons in the word processing module of AppleWorks. When you click a push button the button appears as though it had been pushed in (see Figure 2.14).

- To use a push button, just click the button.

- To undo a push-button action, click the button again.

Pop up list buttons

Pop up list buttons have a small triangle on them. This triangle is the sign that a menu appears when this type of button is clicked (see Figure 2.15). Pop up list buttons are also known as drowp-down list buttons.

Word processing menus

There are eight menus in the word processing menu bar. These menus contain all of the commands needed for word processing (see Figures 2.16 and 2.17)

File menu—This menu manages files. You use it to open and save documents, to insert files into the current document, to create passwords, to record macros, to perform a mail merge, and to print documents.

Edit menu—This menu provides editing functions such as cutting, copying, and pasting text. You may also insert the date, time, and page numbers from this menu. (see Figure 2.18).

Format menu—This menu controls paragraph spacing, line spacing, tabs, footnotes, headers, footers and page breaks.

Font menu—This menu changes the typeface (see Figure 2.19).

Size menu—The size menu controls the size of a font. To change the font size, highlight the type first. The best size for general readability is 11 point, although 10 point is a small, but still readable type, and 12 point is considered a large readable type.

Style menu—The Style menu adds underline, double-underline, italic, strikeout, or other font characteristics to typing. In order to use styles, first highlight the type, then select the appropriate style from the Style menu.

Outline menu—This menu allows you to assign and view different levels of text in an outline form.

Window menu—Use the Window menu to switch between different documents that are open at the same time.

Figure 2.16 The Windows 95 main menu bar.

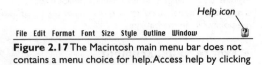

Figure 2.17 The Macintosh main menu bar does not contains a menu choice for help. Access help by clicking on the Help icon.

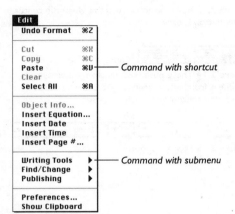

Figure 2.18 The Edit menu contains commands, shortcuts, and commands with submenus.

Sans Serif font
Serif font

Figure 2.19 Sans Serif fonts do not have little tails on the letters, whereas Serif fonts possess decorative tails.

The Windows 95 main menu bar contains a shortcut.
When you see a letter of a menu underlined, such as
File, hold down the left Alt key on the keyboard and
tap the underlined letter. The menu then appears.

File   Edit   Format   Font   Size   Style   Outline   Window   Help

Figure 2.20 The AppleWorks main menu bar for
Windows 95.

Using menus

Menus are the most basic way of accessing
commands in any program.

To uss a menu:

1. Place the tip of the mouse pointer on top
   of the menu you want to use.

2. Hold the mouse button down and the
   menu drops down. There is a list of menu
   items on the left side of the menu and a
   list of shortcuts on the right side of the
   menu.

3. Drag the pointer to the command on the
   list that you want to use and release the
   mouse button.

Windows 95 users may also hold down
the left Alt key and tap the underlined letter
of the menu choice. For example, pressing
Alt+F opens the File menu (see Figure 2.20).

USING MENUS

Document summary

The document summary function is for information about the document that can be used later to help find that document.

To use document summary information:

1. Choose Document Summary from the File menu. The Document Summary dialog box appears (see Figure 2.21).

2. Enter the title of the document, author, version, keywords needed for searching, category, and a brief description of the document.

3. Click the OK button when you are done.

Setting a Password

Document Summary also allows you to set passwords for a document.

To set a password:

1. Choose Document Summary from the file menu. The Document Summary dialog box appears.

2. Click the Set Password button. The password dialog box appears (see Figure 2.22).

3. Type a password in the Password box. The password does not appear on the screen— a series of bullets appears in place of the password.

4. Click the OK button when you are done.

✔ Tip

■ Be careful with passwords. If you use the same password for everything, someone might figure out the password for all your documents. The best passwords contain numbers as well as letters. Do not write passwords down in an easily accessible place. I use a Chinese dictionary to look up good words to use for a password.

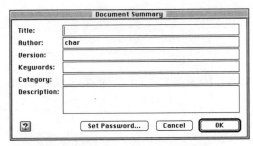

Figure 2.21 The Document Summary dialog box.

Figure 2.22 Passwords appear as bullets when you type them so that no one else can see the password.

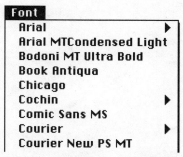

Font
> Arial ▶
> Arial MTCondensed Light
> Bodoni MT Ultra Bold
> Book Antiqua
> Chicago
> Cochin ▶
> Comic Sans MS
> Courier ▶
> Courier New PS MT

Figure 2.23 The Font menu. Available fonts are slightly different for Windows 95 machines and the Macintosh. If you need to exchange documents regularly between a Macintosh and a Windows 95 machine, use only Arial and Times Roman as main fonts. Helvetica is equivalent to Arial; Times and Times Roman are equivalent serif fonts.

Size
> 9 Point
> 10 Point
> ✓ 12 Point
> 14 Point
> 18 Point
> 24 Point
> 36 Point
> 48 Point
> 72 Point
>
> Other... ⇧⌘0
> Smaller ⇧⌘<
> Larger ⇧⌘>

Figure 2.24 The Size menu.

Initial font

The last step in setting up any new document is to chose the initial font:

1. Click at the top of the opening page of the new word processing document. The cursor appears as a vertical blinking line.

2. To choose the font, click the Font menu at the top of the main menu bar. The Font menu appears (see Figure 2.23).

3. Click the font you want to use.

4. Click the Size menu at the top of the main menu bar to choose the font size. The Size menu appears (see Figure 2.24).

Font, Size, and Style menus appear in two places in AppleWorks. The main menu bar contains Font, Size, and Style items. These choices also appear in the toolbar.

To use the toolbar buttons, click the appropriate button. The menu associated with that button appears.

✔ Tip

■ Average size type for reading is 11 point. Here are examples of the three main text type sizes:

Size 10
Size 11
Size 12

Continue on to Chapter 3, "First Documents," to learn more about formatting and creating your first word processing documents.

INITIAL FONT

FIRST DOCUMENTS

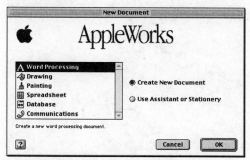

Figure 3.1 The AppleWorks Opening dialog box.

Ready to start the first document? The first few steps are the same for both Macintosh and Windows95 users:

1. Start AppleWorks by double-clicking the AppleWorks icon. The Opening dialog box appears (see Figure 3.1).

2. Choose Word Processing from the opening dialog box.

3. Select the New Document radio button. The Word Processing screen appears.

Setting up a document

Before you start typing you need to decide:

- Size of paper on which your document is to be printed

- Margins you need for the document

- A typeface for the document

- Whether you want to have page numbers

Setting the paper size is a little different for Windows 95 users than for Macintosh users. The next few pages are dedicated to Windows 95 users. Macintosh users should skip ahead to "Macintosh Page Setup" on page 34 for directions how to begin setting up the document.

Windows 95 Print setup

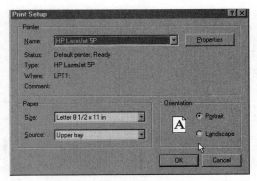

Figure 3.2 The Print Setup dialog box.

Standard paper in the United States is 8.5 by 11 inches. Before you begin writing the document, change all printer settings you need to change in order to make the printer work with this new document.

1. Choose Print Setup from the File menu. The Print Setup dialog box appears (see Figure 3.2). This dialog box has three panes: Printer pane, Paper pane, and Orientation pane.

2. Click the Name of the printer you want to use in the pop up menu of the Printer pane.

3. Choose the appropriate printer from the drop-down menu.

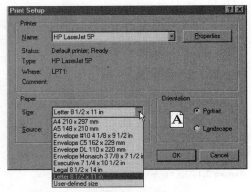

Figure 3.3 The paper settings tab in the Print Properties dialog box. Click the appropriate paper icon at the top of the dialog box in the Paper size menu.

To change the paper size:

1. Choose the size pop up menu in the Paper pane (see Figure 3.3).

2. Choose the paper size you want to use from the size pop up menu.

When printing letterhead or envelopes, select the appropriate Source in the Paper pane (see Figure 3.4).

Figure 3.4 Many printers have additional options for the paper, such as this dialog box for the HP4Plus. When you need to use special paper or envelopes you can choose Manual feed and then insert the special paper or envelope by hand.

Figure 3.5 These four tabs at the top of the Print Properties dialog box contain settings that apply to the printer. Click a tab to see settings that are currently being used.

To change the paper orientation:

1. Click the Portrait or Landscape radio button.

2. Click the OK button when you are finished.

Paper that is in landscape orientation does not need to be placed into the printer in any different fashion. The printer takes care of making the fonts print lengthwise on the paper without you having to turn the paper sidewise in the print.

Properties button

The Print Setup dialog box contains a properties button that allows you to make more sophisticated changes to the document and the printer, including making the printer work correctly with the paper, fonts and graphics (see Figure 3.5).

Now, skip ahead to "Changing Margins" on page 35.

WINDOWS 95 PRINT SETUP

Macintosh Page setup

You need to make sure the Macintosh printer works with the paper you are using for the documents and that you are connected to the appropriate printer.

To change the page setup:

1. Choose Page Setup from the File menu. The Page Setup Dialog box appears (see Figure 3.6).

2. Click the Paper pop up menu in the Page Setup dialog box. The Paper pop up menu appears.

3. Choose the type of paper to be used with this document.

4. Choose any Page Setup options, reduction or enlargement options, or click on the appropriate Orientation button.

5. Click the OK button when you are finished.

✔ Tip

■ Page setup is slightly different for each type of printer. Consult the manual for your printer to make sure you understand the options presented to you in the Page Setup dialog box.

Figure 3.6 This is the Page Setup dialog box for a LaserWriter. If you own a different printer, this box may appear with different options.

Figure 3.7 The Format menu contains categories of formatting options:

Document... for setting margins and document display options

Rulers... for setting ruler measurement in inches, centimeters, picas, or points

Section... for setting page numbers, columns and headers or footers

Paragraph... for setting indentions, line spacing, alignment and space before or after a paragraph

Tab... for setting tabs, dot leaders, and type of tab (left, center, right, or decimal)

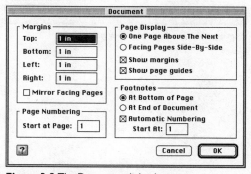

Figure 3.8 The Document dialog box.

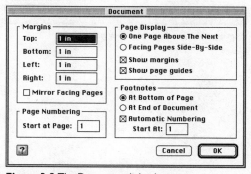

Figure 3.9 The Page Display panel in the Document dialog box.

Changing margins

Standard margins on all documents are 1 inch on the top, bottom, left and right. You may need different margins for the document.

To change margins:

1. Choose Document from the Format menu. The Document dialog box appears (see Figures 3.7 and 3.8).

2. In the Margins dialog box, type the top, bottom, left and right margins to be used.

3. Click the OK button when you are finished.

Not all printers print out to the very edge of the paper. If you have set the margins closer to the paper edge than the printer can print, words and letters will appear cut off on the printed document.

Use the Tab key to move between the margin entry boxes. Type the measurement you want to use for the top margin, for example, then tap the Tab key to move to the bottom margin entry box. Continue using the Tab key to move between margin entry boxes. Shift+Tab moves you backwards between margin entry boxes.

Miscellaneous settings

You can change how the document is displayed by clicking the Facing Pages side by side radio button in the Page Display pane of the Document dialog box (see Figure 3.9).

Facing pages are when a document appears on the screen like an open book, with one page appearing on the left and the second page appearing on the right.

Page numbering

Page numbering appears in either the footer or the header of the document. Other text may also be added to the footer or header in addition to a page number.

Creating page numbers

1. Choose Insert Header or Insert Footer from the format menu. The header or footer area appears as two light gray lines with a blank line where you can type.

2. Choose Insert Page # from the Edit menu. (Be careful not to click outside the header area before you perform this step.)

You may choose page number, section number, section page count, or document page count. Page counts refer to the total number of pages in the section or in the document (see Figure 3.10).

Changing page numbers

If you want to change page numbers in the middle of the document or if you with to begin the document with a page number other than the number one, you need to use the Section command on the Format menu.

To begin the document with a number other than the number one:

1. Choose Section from the Format menu. The Section dialog box appears (see Figure 3.11).

2. Choose Restart Page Number from the Page Number pane of the Section dialog box.

3. Click the OK button when you are finished.

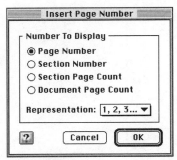

Figure 3.10 Most page numbering uses Arabic numbering. You may number the pages using Arabic numbers, capital Roman numbers, lower-case Roman numbers, or upper-case or lower-case letters from the Representation pop up menu.

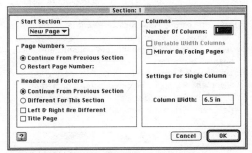

Figure 3.11 The Section dialog box.

Changing appearance of page numbers

To change the appearance of a page number:

1. Highlight the page number you want to change.

2. Choose the font, size, and style characteristics you want to use.

✔ Tip

- If you change the appearance of a page number on one page, the appearance changes on all pages of the document.

Removing page numbers

1. Click inside of the header or footer that contains the page numbers.

2. Choose Remove Header (or Footer) from the Format menu. Your page numbers disappear.

Fonts and font sizes

Fonts are the basis of word processing. The term *font* refers to the typeface, size, and style of type. Typeface refers to the name of the type, such as Arial or Times.

Changing the font

To change the font for a word, paragraph, page, or the entire document:

1. Highlight the text you want to change.

2. Open the Font menu. The Font menu lists appears (see Figure 3.12).

3. Choose the font you want to use from the Font menu, or use the Other menu choice to choose fonts that do not appear on the Font menu.

To change the font size:

To change the size of a font for a word, paragraph, page, or the entire document:

1. Highlight the text you want to change.

2. Open the Size menu (see Figure 3.13).

3. Choose the size you want to use from the Size menu, or choose Larger or Smaller to make the highlighted font slightly larger or smaller.

✔ Tip

■ Use the Size pop up menu on the ruler bar. This pop up menu gives you faster access to font, style, size, and color choices (see Figure 3.14).

Figure 3.12 The Font menu.

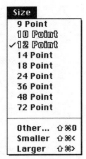

Figure 3.13 The Size menu.

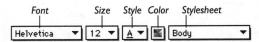

Figure 3.14 Useful buttons on the ruler bar.

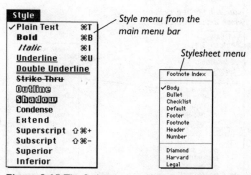

Style menu from the main menu bar

Stylesheet menu

Figure 3.15 The Style menu on the main menu bar is completely different from the Stylesheet menu on the toolbar. Don't confuse these two. Styles refers to font styles such as bold; Stylesheets refers to multiple types of formatting such as small font with a bullet.

Superior   Superscript   Subscript

The sky in ^{F}indlay ^{O}hio is full of H$_2$O

Figure 3.16 Superior and superscript, inferior, and subscript all raise the type above the main text, or lower the type below the main text. Superior raises the font and makes the type much smaller than superscript. Inferior lowers the font and makes the type smaller than subscript.

Adding styles to fonts

Styles refer to textual enhancements such as bold, italic or underline. In this version of AppleWorks you may use:

- Plain text
- Bold
- Italic
- Underline
- Double underline
- Strike Thru
- Superscript
- Subscript
- Superior
- Inferior

To use a font style

1. Highlight the text you want to change.

2. Choose Style from the main menu bar (see Figures 3.15 and 3.16).

3. Choose the style you want to use from the Style menu.

Removing a font style

If you change your mind and do not want to use a particular style, you must turn the style off by repeating the same steps that you performed to turn the style on. See the instructions above for using a font style for an example.

Using stylesheets

Stylesheets aren't related to the Style menu. Stylesheets are a fast way to apply attributes such as bullets or header styles. You can use stylesheets to turn text into a footnote, header, or list with bullets, boxes, or check list boxes (see Figure 3.17).

To use a stylesheet:

1. Highlight the text you wish to change.

2. Select the stylesheet you wish to use from the Stylesheet pop up menu.

Text color

If you have a color printer, printing the text in color makes the document look beautiful. With AppleWorks, this is easy to do.

To make the text have color:

1. Highlight the text you want to make a color.

2. Click the Quick Access color button. The color palette appears (see Figure 3.18).

3. Click the color on the palette you want to use with the text.

Tips on color overheads

Color takes a long time to print. Often the colored ink in the printer isn't transparent and when you use it on an overhead, all that can be seen is black. Color makes great handouts though, particularly if you adhere to good rules of contrast:

■ Yellow or white text on a black or dark blue background make the best contrast.

■ Other good choices include cyan text on black or navy blue, white text on dark red, or yellow on dark green.

Notice the light grey line which indicates the margin

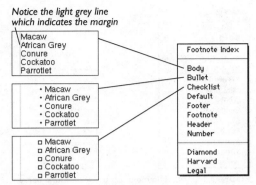

Figure 3.17 The same list formatted with three different stylesheets.

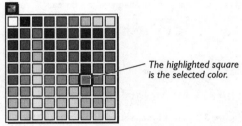

The highlighted square is the selected color.

Figure 3.18 This is the color palette. Move the cursor over the palette until the color you want is surrounded by a dark line, then let go of the mouse button.

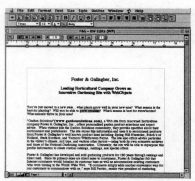

Figure 3.19 Highlighting a few words.

Figure 3.20 To select all of the text in an entire document, choose Select All under the Edit menu. Or press ⌘-A on the Macintosh, Control+A on Windows 95.

Figure 3.21 Many of the Edit commands are on the Button Bar. Here is the Cut button. Cut text is removed from the document and placed in the Clipboard, where you may re-use it later.

Editing text

In order to make changes to a document, you need to highlight or select text. There are several ways to highlight text:

- To highlight a word, position the pointer in the word and double-click.

- To highlight a paragraph, position the pointer in the paragraph and triple-click.

- Click at the beginning of the first word you want to highlight. Hold the Shift key down. Click at the end of the last word you want to highlight. Let go of the Shift key. (see Figure 3.19)

- Position the pointer in front of the first word you want to highlight. Hold the mouse button down and drag over the words you want to highlight. Release the button.

- Drag the mouse pointer down the side of the page until all lines of text you want to highlight are selected.

- You can also highlight the entire document by choosing Select All on the Edit menu, or pressing ⌘-A on the Macintosh, or Control+A on Windows 95 systems (see Figure 3.20).

Highlighted text

Once you highlight or select text, you can perform a variety of functions on the text:

- Delete the text by pressing the delete or clear key

- Change the font, size or style

- Cut the text (see Figure 3.21).

- Copy the text

- Type over the text

EDITING TEXT

Alignment

There are four types of alignment:

- Left—Text is aligned on the left, ragged on the right. This is the normal setting for most text.

- Center—Text is in the center between the left and right margins.

- Right—Text is aligned on the right, ragged on the left. This is used in newsletters, to set the date in a letter to the right, and for fancy text like poetry.

- Justified—Text is aligned on both the left and right side. This option does not look good unless you also hyphenate the text. Also known as full alignment.

To change text alignment:

1. Highlight the text you want to align.

2. Click the left, center, right, or full alignment button on the ruler bar (see Figure 3.22).

Figure 3.22 The text-alignment buttons on the ruler bar.

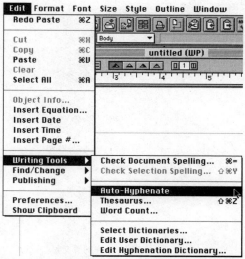

Figure 3.23 Turning Auto-Hyphenation on. There is no shortcut key for Auto-Hyphenation.

Along·came·the·fabulous·Severe·ma-caw,·Sweetpea.·She·really·is·a·case!·Not·only·is·Sweetpea·the·greediest·little·piggy·but·she·is·the·most·asser-tive,·cutest,·and·playful·Severe·I've·ever·seen.¶

Figure 3.24 Detail of file with full alignment and hyphenation on.

Along· came· the· fabulous· Severe·macaw,· Sweetpea.· She· really· is· a·case!· Not· only· is· Sweetpea· the·greediest· little· piggy· but· she· is· the·most· assertive,· cutest,· and· playful·Severe·I've·ever·seen.¶

Figure 3.25 Detail of file with full alignment and hyphenation off. Notice the larger gaps between words.

Along·came·the·fabulous·Severe·macaw,·Sweetpea.·She·really·is·a·case!·Not·only·is·Sweetpea·the·greediest·little·piggy·but·she·is·the·most·assertive,·cutest,·and·playful·Severe·I've·ever·seen.¶

Figure 3.26 Detail of file with left alignment and hyphenation off.

Hyphenating text

If you want to use Full alignment, make sure you hyphenate the text to make it look better.

To hyphenate:

1. Open the file which you want to hyphen-ate.

2. Click anywhere in the text of the docu-ment.

3. Choose Auto-Hyphenate from the Writing Tools submenu on the edit menu. Hyphenation is automatically turned on (see Figure 3.23).

Auto-Hyphenation is a toggle. When you turn Auto-Hyphenation on, a checkmark appears by the menu entry. When you turn Auto-Hyphenation off, the checkmark disappears and hyphenation disappears from the document.

For samples of how hyphenation looks with full and left alignment, see Figures 3.24 through 3.26.

✔ Tip

■ When Auto-Hyphenation is turned on, it is turned on for the entire document. It is not possible to auto-hyphenate just a por-tion of the text.

HYPHENATING TEXT

INTERMEDIATE WORD PROCESSING

4

This chapter introduces concepts that help you manage word processing in an easier fashion.

In this chapter you will learn easier ways of editing text; how to use advanced formatting options for documents, sections, and paragraphs; how to set tabs; and how to use automatic insert features.

Moving and inserting text

You have already learned how to cut text, which removes text from the document. You may also cut text and place it in the document in a different position. You may also use the Copy command to make a copy of text and place that text in a different position or multiple positions within a document.

To move text:

1. Highlight the text you want to move.

2. Choose Cut from the Edit menu if you want to remove the text from its original position,

   or

   Choose Copy from the Edit menu if you want the text to repeat in another position (see Figure 4.1).

3. Click where you want to place the text.

4. Choose Paste from the Edit menu. The text appears in the document.

The Clipboard

Where does cut or copied text go?

Cut or copied text is saved on a clipboard utility that comes with both Macintosh and Windows 95 machines. Text is saved on the clipboard as long as you have not cut or copied anything else. The clipboard can only keep track of one item at a time.

Macintosh users can choose Show Clipboard from the Edit menu to see what's in the clipboard (see Figures 4.2 and 4.3).

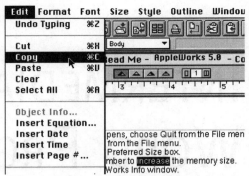

Figure 4.1 Copying text. The highlighted text can be either Cut or Copied, then used again, by inserting the text using the Paste command. If you choose Clear, the text will be erased.

Figure 4.2 Choosing Show Clipboard from the Edit menu on a Macintosh.

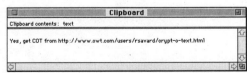

Figure 4.3 The Clipboard. Here's the last item that was copied or cut.

Figure 4.4 Find/Change has the shortcut ⌘-F on the Macintosh or Control+F on Windows 95. You find the same word again without using all of the steps you used to find the word the first time by pressing ⌘-E on the Macintosh, or Control+E on Windows 95.

If you only want to find something and don't wish to make changes you don't need to fill out the Change box.

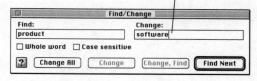

Figure 4.5 The Find/Change dialog box on Macintosh. Here we're searching for the word "product" and changing it to "software."

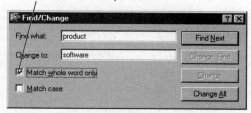

Figure 4.6 The word "product" was found in the text. You can tell it was found because the word is now outlined.

To avoid changing words that might include the word you are looking for—such as changing "productivity" when you are looking for "product"—click the Match whole word only checkbox.

Figure 4.7 The Find/Change dialog box in Windows 95.

Find/Change commands

Find and Change commands are sometimes called Find and Replace. Find is used to locate a particular word or phrase. Change can used to replace the found words or phrases.

To use Find

1. Choose Find/Change from the Find/Change... submenu of the Edit menu (see Figure 4.4) or press ⌘-F on the Macintosh or Control+F on Windows 95. The Find/Change dialog box appears.

2. Type the text you are looking for in the Find box of the Find/Change dialog box (see Figure 4.5).

3. Click the Find Next button. The word is found and appears with an outline surrounding it (see Figure 4.6).

To change text

1. Choose Find/Change from the Find/Change... submenu of the Edit menu. The Find/Change dialog box appears (see Figure 4.7).

2. Type the text you are looking for in the Find box.

3. Type the new text you want to use in the Change box.

4. Click the Find Next button to locate the first occurrence.

5. Click the Change button to replace the found text. Or click the Change, Find button to change the found text and locate the next instance. Or click the Change All button to change all instances in the text at once.

✔ Tip

- Use Change All with caution. You cannot Undo changes made with Change All.

FIND/CHANGE COMMANDS

Limiting the search

You can limit where Find looks in the document:

To limit a Find command:

1. Highlight the text you want to search.

2. Choose Find/Change from the Edit menu, or use the appropriate shortcut key.

3. Type the word you want to find in the Find box.

4. Click the Find Next button.

AppleWorks searches only in the highlighted text.

Special characters

It's easy to type text in the Find box, but to look for a special character or text command (such as Date), you must search using codes, as shown in Table 4.1.

Table 4.1

Finding Special Characters	
SPECIAL CHARACTER	**CHARACTERS TO TYPE IN THE FIND BOX**
Automatic Date	\d
Automatic Time	\h
Page numbers	\#
Tab	\t
Return or enter	\p
Soft return (Shift+Enter)	\N
End of column	\c
End of page	\c

Click where you want the date to appear. If you need a blank line, press the Enter key to create the blank line, then press the Up arrow to get back onto that blank line quickly.

11/1/97

Dear David Butler:

It's been a long time. Thirty-two years to be exact.

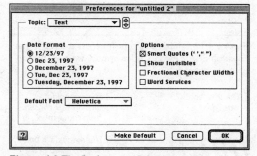

Figure 4.8 Insert options on the Edit menu. Notice there are no shortcuts for these options.

Figure 4.9 The Preferences dialog box.

1:20 PM

Figure 4.10 The computer picks up the time from the BIOS chip inside of the computer. Make sure the time on your computer is set correctly.

Inserting automatic text

AppleWorks allows you to insert date, time, and page numbers automatically. For more information on page numbers, see "Page numbering" in this chapter.

To insert the date

1. Click where you want the date to appear in the text.

2. Choose Insert Date from the Edit menu. The date appears where you clicked (see Figure 4.8).

To change the format of the date

The date might not appear in the format you want.

1. Select Preferences from the Edit menu. The Preferences dialog box appears (see Figure 4.9).

2. Click the radio button for the date format you want to use.

Dates that were input into the document using the Insert Date command change format automatically. But if you typed a date manually, it will not change format.

To insert the time

Inserting the time works exactly like inserting the date.

1. Click where you want the time to appear in the text.

2. Choose Insert Time from the Edit menu. The time appears where you clicked (see Figure 4.10).

Unlike dates, you cannot change the format of times that you have inserted into a document.

Equations

You do not need to struggle with creating equations in AppleWorks. The Insert Equation function gives you the capability of creating any type of advanced math equation.

To create an equation:

1. Click in the text where you want the equation to appear.

2. Choose Insert Equation from the Edit menu. The Equation Editor utility appears in a separate window. This is not a dialog box, but is actually a miniature program that runs along with AppleWorks (see Figure 4.11).

3. Click the Equation symbol set you want to use. The pop-up menu appears.

4. Click the Symbol on the symbol set pop-up menu that you want to use (see Figure 4.12).

5. Type the text or numbers you want to input along with the symbol set (see Figure 4.13).

6. Choose Close from the File menu. The new equation appears in the body of the main text.

Macintosh Equation Editor

When you use Equation Editor on a Macintosh, the main menu bar in AppleWorks changes to the Macintosh Equation Editor menu bar. When you're all finished creating equations in your AppleWorks document, choose Quit from the File menu of the Equation Editor to quit the Equation Editor utility program.

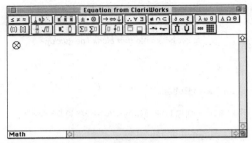

Figure 4.11 The Equation Editor.

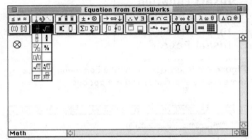

Figure 4.12 Symbol sets appear across the top of the Equation Editor menu. Click a symbol set, and the pop-up menu appears.

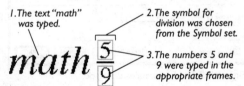

1. The text "math" was typed.

2. The symbol for division was chosen from the Symbol set.

3. The numbers 5 and 9 were typed in the appropriate frames.

Figure 4.13 The math symbols contain frames where you can type numbers.

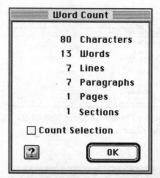

Figure 4.14 To see how many words are in your document, choose Word Count from the Writing Tools submenu in the Edit menu.

Figure 4.15 The Spelling utility offers alternatives for words it thinks are misspelled.

Writing tools

The Edit menu contains Writing tools designed to make producing documents with AppleWorks easy. Writing Tools include:

- Spelling

- Hyphenation (see "Hyphenating text" in Chapter 3)

- Thesaurus

- Word Count (see Figure 4.14)

Spelling

To check spelling in a AppleWorks document:

1. Open the document you want to spell check.

2. Choose Check Document Spelling from the Writing Tools command on the Edit menu. The Spelling dialog box appears.

3. Once the Spelling utility stops on a word and indicates that it is spelled incorrectly, the word appears in the Word box at the top of the Spelling dialog box. (see Figure 4.15)

4. Choose a replacement word from the Spelling list and click the Replace button. You can use the shortcut keys on the left side of the Spelling list to choose the replacement word.
   or
   Click the Skip button if the word is spelled correctly.
   or
   Click the Learn button if you want to add the word to the spelling dictionary.

5. Click the Cancel button to stop spell checking, or click the Done button. (The Cancel button becomes the Done button when the entire document has been checked.)

Thesaurus

Sometimes it's handy to have a reference to look up alternative words when you are writing. AppleWorks furnishes a fine thesaurus for you to use.

To use Thesaurus:

1. Click anywhere in the text, or highlight a word for which you want to find a synonym.

2. Choose Thesaurus from the Writing Tools command on the Edit menu. The Thesaurus dialog box appears (see Figure 4.16).

3. If you highlighted a word, a list of alternative words appears in the Thesaurus dialog box. Click any word you want to use in the Thesaurus dialog box.

4. Click the Replace button. The word appears instead of the high lighted word and the Thesaurus dialog box automatically closes.

If you did not highlight a word before you selected Thesaurus from the Writing Tools command on the Edit menu, an empty Thesaurus dialog box appears.

To look up a word:

1. Type the word you want to look up in the Find box at the bottom of the Thesaurus dialog box (see Figures 4.17 and 4.18).

2. Click the Lookup button. A list of words appears in the Thesaurus dialog box.

3. Click the word you want to use in the Thesaurus dialog box.

4. Click the Replace button. The word appears in the body of the text and the Thesaurus dialog box automatically closes.

Find box   Word list

Figure 4.16 To open the Thesaurus, press Shift-⌘-Z on the Macintosh. On Windows 95 machines, press Shift+Control+Z.

Figure 4.17 When you look up a word in the Thesaurus dialog box, the list indicates what part of speech alternative words are.

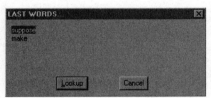

Figure 4.18 If you want to see what other words you have previously looked up using Thesaurus, click the Last Word button in the Thesaurus dialog box. The Last Words dialog box appears. You may then select a word from the Last Words list and click the lookup button to look that word up.

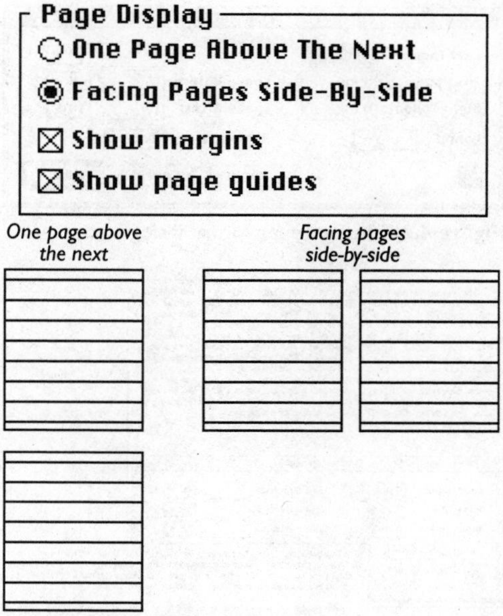

```
┌─ Page Display ──────────────────────┐
│  ○ One Page Above The Next          │
│  ◉ Facing Pages Side-By-Side        │
│  ⊠ Show margins                     │
│  ⊠ Show page guides                 │
└─────────────────────────────────────┘
```

One page above   Facing pages
the next   side-by-side

Figure 4.19 Page Display options.

The Format menu

The Format menu lets you set options for how the document appears, paragraph indentations and spaces both before and after, and tab settings.

Document format

Document format on the Format menu controls Margins, Page Display and Footnotes. To understand how to setup margins, see "Changing margins" in Chapter 3. For information on footnotes, see "Inserting footnotes" and "Removing footnotes" later in this chapter.

Page Display

Page Display controls how the page looks on the screen. This can be important if you are trying to desktop publish a document and appearance is important.

To set the page display:

1. Choose Document from the Format menu.

2. Click the radio button for the type of screen display you want to use.

3. Click the OK button when you are finished.

✔ Tip

- Facing pages side-by-side is best if you are creating a book (see Figure 4.19).

THE FORMAT MENU

Paragraph formatting

Many people still press Return twice between paragraphs. That's extra work! By changing the spacing between each paragraph, you can just press the Return key once and still have an extra blank line space between each paragraph.

Line spacing

To change line spacing within paragraphs:

1. Before you start typing, click in the document. If you have already started typing and you want to change the line spacing within all paragraphs, choose Select All under the Edit menu to highlight the paragraphs you have already typed.

2. Choose Paragraph from the Format menu. The Paragraph dialog box appears (see Figure 4.20).

3. Click the Line Spacing box and type how much space you want between lines within each paragraph. The default number is 1 (single-spaced).

4. Click the OK button when you are finished.

Paragraph spacing

To change spacing between paragraphs:

1. Before you start typing, click in the document. If you have already started typing and you want to change the space between all paragraphs, choose Select All under the Edit menu to highlight the paragraphs you have already typed.

2. Choose Paragraph from the Format menu. The Paragraph dialog box appears.

3. Click the Space After box and type how many *extra* line spaces you want between paragraphs (see Figure 4.21).

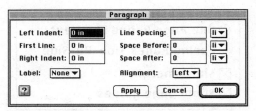

Figure 4.20 The Paragraph format dialog box.

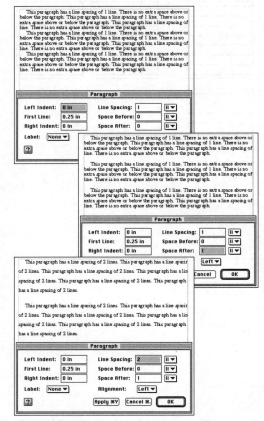

Figure 4.21 Adding space between paragraphs.

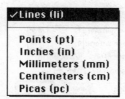

Figure 4.22 The Measurement pop-up menu.

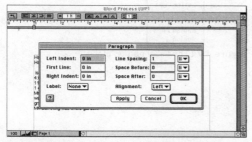

Figure 4.23 You can change Alignment settings in the Paragraph dialog box or by using the buttons on the Ruler bar.

Measurement systems

If you prefer to define line- and paragraph spacing in points, inches, millimeters, centimeters, or picas, you may use those measurement methods in the Paragraph dialog box (see Figure 4.22)

To change measurement systems:

1. Choose Paragraph from the Format menu. The Paragraph dialog box appears.

2. Click the measurement pop-up menu on the right side of the measurement you want to change.

3. Choose the measurement option you want to use.

Alignment

There are Style and Alignment buttons on the ruler bar, but they also appear in the Paragraph dialog box. You can use either the buttons on the ruler bar or the commands in the Paragraph dialog box to set or change Styles and Alignment (see Figure 4.23).

To change the Alignment:

1. Highlight the text you want to change.

2. Choose Paragraph from the Format menu. The Paragraph dialog box appears.

3. Click the Alignment pop-up menu.

4. Choose the alignment you want to use (Left, Center, Right, or Justify).

5. Click the OK button when you are finished.

Label

The Label feature automatically provides bullets, checkboxes, numbers, or Roman numerals at the beginning of paragraphs.

To use a Label:

1. Highlight the text you want to label.

2. Choose Paragraph from the Format menu. The Paragraph dialog box appears.

3. Click the Label pop-up menu (see Figure 4.24).

4. Choose the kind of label you want to use (Legal, Letter, Numeric, Checkbox, Bullet, etc.).

5. Click the OK button when you are done.

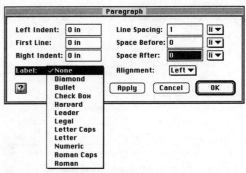

Figure 4.24 The Label pop-up menu.

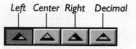

Figure 4.25 The Tab buttons in the Ruler bar.

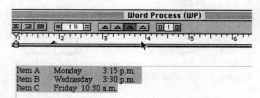

Figure 4.26 Click on the Ruler to place a tab.

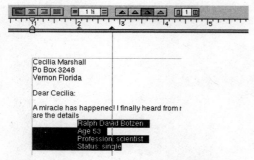

Figure 4.27 A light gray vertical line shows when you move a tab. This line may be used as a measuring device for proper tab positioning.

Figure 4.28 Removing a tab.

Adding tabs

Settings tabs in AppleWorks is easy because you set the tabs by clicking in the ruler wherever you want a tab to appear.

To set tabs

If you have already typed text, and you want to add tabs, highlight the text before you follow steps below.

1. Click on the left, right, center, or decimal tab button on the Ruler bar (see Figure 4.25).

2. Click in the ruler where you want the tab to appear (see Figure 4.26).

Moving tabs

1. Move the mouse pointer on top of the tab on the ruler bar that you want to move.

2. Hold the mouse button down and drag the tab to the new position (see Figure 4.27).

3. Release the mouse button.

Removing tabs

1. Select the tab on the ruler bar and drag the tab below the ruler (see Figure 4.28).

TABS

Formatting tabs

There is also an option on the Format menu for setting tabs. To use this option:

1. Choose Tab from the Format menu. The Tab dialog box appears (see Figure 4.29).

2. In the Alignment box, choose the type of tab you want to place.

3. In the Position box, type the tab placement.

4. Click on the Apply or the OK button.

Adding leaders to tabs

1. Select the type of alignment you want the tab to have from the radio buttons in the Alignment pane.

2. Type the tab placement in the Position box in the Tab dialog box (see Figure 4.29).

3. Select the radio button in the Fill pane for the type of leader you want to use.

4. Click the OK button when you are finished.

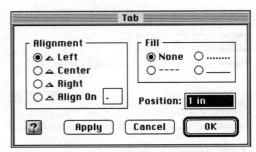

Figure 4.29 The Tab dialog box.

Name	Number	Species	Price
Velcro	789	Molaccun	$1200
Bubi	87-988	B/G macaw	$1500
Yingwu	876553	WH Caique	$1000
Sweetpea	76756	Severe Macaw	$950
Jabri	678077	African Grey	$1200

Figure 4.30 This ruler has four different types of tabs on it as well as margins. To use this ruler and the tab settings click the text with these tabs. Copy the ruler. Now click the text where you want to use this ruler, and Apply the ruler.

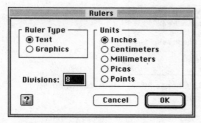

Figure 4.31 Text ruler settings.

Ruler format

Rulers display information about the basic format of text, including tabs and indents. You can copy tab information by copying a ruler (see Figures 4.30 and 4.31).

Copying rulers

To copy a ruler:

1. Click the text that contains the ruler information you want to use.

2. Choose Copy Ruler from the Format menu (press Shift-⌘-C on the Macintosh or Shift+Control+C on Windows 95).

3. The ruler is copied. Now you must apply the ruler.

Applying rulers

To apply the ruler:

1. Click the place in the text where you want to use the ruler you just copied.

2. Choose Apply Ruler from the Format menu (press Shift-⌘-V on the Macintosh or Shift+Control+V on Windows 95).

3. The ruler appears in the document.

Rulers on the Format menu

You may specify the measurement system for any ruler:

1. Choose Ruler from the Format menu. The Rulers dialog box appears.

2. Click the type of measurement increments you desire in the ruler in the Units pane (see Figure 4.31).

3. Click the OK button when you are done.

RULER FORMAT

Footnotes

Inserting a footnote

1. Click immediately after the word to which you want to attach a footnote (see Figure 4.32).

2. Choose Insert Footnote from the Format menu (press Shift-⌘-F on the Macintosh or Shift+Control+F on Windows 95) (see Figure 4.33).

3. Type the footnote. Footnote numbers are created automatically (see Figure 4.34).

Removing footnotes

1. Find the footnote number in the body text and highlight it.

2. Press the Delete key.

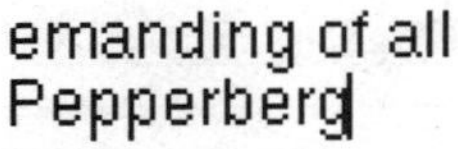

emanding of all
Pepperberg

Figure 4.32 Click just after the word where you want to insert a footnote.

Figure 4.33 Choose Insert Footnote from the Format menu.

---
[1] Dr Irene Pepperberg works out of the University of Arizona an African Grey.

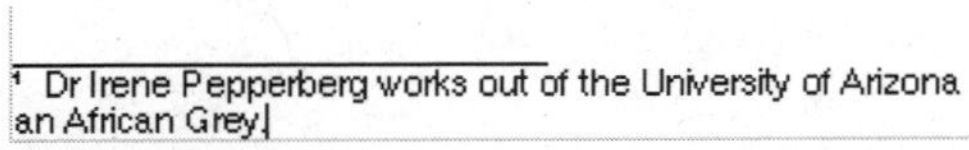

Figure 4.34 Footnotes automatically number themselves and automatically draw a line between the footnote text and the body text of the document.

Figure 4.35 Once you have inserted a header, the Insert Header command on the Format menu changes to Remove Header.

Headers and footers

Inserting headers and footers

Headers and footers are repeating text that appears on the top or bottom of a page. Headers and footers may contain:

- Page numbers
- Inserted date or time
- Typed text
- Graphics

To insert a continuous header or footer:

1. With the cursor anywhere in the document, choose Insert Header or Insert Footer from the Format menu. The cursor appears inside a header or footer that is one line deep (see Figure 4.35).

2. Change the font, size, or style of type for the header or footer by highlighting the text and using the appropriate menu.

3. Type the text for the header or footer. You can place page numbers in a header or footer by choosing Insert Page #... from the Edit menu.

4. Click in the main portion of the document. The header or footer now appears on every page.

To remove a header:

1. Click anywhere on a page that contains the header you want to remove.

2. Choose Remove Header from the Format menu. This removes the header from all pages in a section.

HEADERS AND FOOTERS

Multiple headers or footers

It is possible to have one header, then switch to another header. This situation is common with books and pamphlets.

To change headers or footers in the middle of the document:

1. In the open document, create the first header or footer you want to use.

2. Click at the top of the page where you want a different type of header or footer to appear.

3. Choose Insert Section from the Format menu. This creates an invisible section mark.

4. Choose Section from the Format menu. The Section dialog box appears (see Figure 4.36).

5. Click the Different For This Section radio button in the Headers and Footers pane of the Section dialog box.

6. Click the OK button when you are done.

7. Type the new header (or footer) in the header region at the top (or bottom) of the page. You might have to delete the text that was there originally to put the new text in place.

✔ Tips

■ To have different headers or footers for left and right pages, click the Left & Right Are Different checkbox. Be sure to also choose Document under the Format menu and click the Facing Pages Side-by-Side radio button.

■ Use the Title Page checkbox to define unique headers or footers for the first page of a document.

Click the Restart Page Number radio button to change the page numbering within a section.

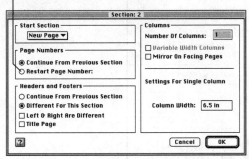

Figure 4.36 Sections can start on a new page or be continuous and break a page into sections without starting a new page. The number in the title bar indicates this is the second section in the document.

Figure 4.37 The Open File dialog box.

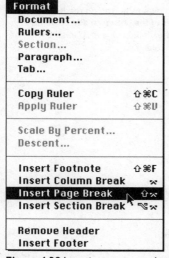

Figure 4.38 Inserting a new page break

Inserting files

Sometimes you need to combine two or more documents. To do this you insert a file.

To insert a file:

1. Click where you want the second file to appear in the document.

2. If you want the file to begin on a new line, press the Return key.

3. Choose Insert from the File menu. The Open File dialog box appears (see Figure 4.37).

4. Choose the file you want to insert.

5. Click the Insert button. The file appears in the document.

Page breaks

If you just keep typing, AppleWorks starts new pages automatically. Sometimes they're not quite where you had in mind. To insert a page break in a specific place:

1. Click where you want to insert the page break.

2. Choose Insert Page Break from the Format menu (see Figure 4.38). The new page appears.

Page breaks leave no signs that they were inserted, other than a new page appearing. If you inserted a page break, however, you can take it out. To remove an unwanted manual page break:

1. Click to the left of the first word following the page break.

2. Press the backspace key if you are on a Windows 95 system or the Delete key if you are on a Macintosh system. The text returns to its automatic pagination, which usually means some text will move up to the previous page.

Columns

You can make text appear in columns throughout a document. This is useful for newsletters.

Inserting columns

To create columns of equal width:

1. Open or create the document you want to contain columns.

2. Click anywhere in the document or, if it has multiple sections, in the section you want to put in columns.

3. Choose Section from the Format menu. The Section dialog box appears (see Figure 4.39).

4. In the Columns pane, type a number in the Number Of Columns box.

5. Click the OK button when you are finished.

AppleWorks divides the area between the margins into columns of equal width.

✔ Tips

- You can adjust the space between columns by entering a value in the Space Between box.

- You can also use the columns buttons on the Ruler bar to create columns (see Figure 4.40).

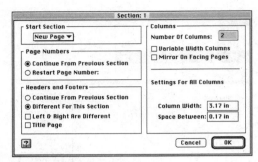

Figure 4.39 The Section dialog box.

Figure 4.40 The columns button on the Ruler bar. Click the right part of the button to add columns. Multiple clicks add multiple columns. Click the left button to remove columns.

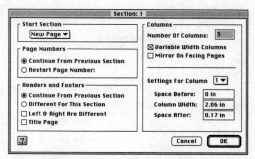

Figure 4.41 Creating columns of varying widths.

Variable-width columns

Columns don't all have to be the same width. You can specify column widths and the amount space between columns in AppleWorks.

To specify column width and spacing:

1. Choose Section from the Format menu.

2. In the Columns pane of the Section dialog box, click the box that says Variable Width Columns (see Figure 4.41).

3. In the Column Width box type the width you want the first column to be.

4. Click the Space Before box and type the amount space you want to the left of the column.

5. Click the Space After box and type the amount of space you want to the right of the column.

6. Click the Settings pop-up menu and choose the next column for which you want to set the width and spacing. Repeat steps 3 through 5 until widths for all columns have been set.

7. Click the OK button when you are done.

COLUMNS

Masteheads and columns

A "masthead" is the title information that runs across the front page of a newspaper. Mastheads span multiple columns. You can create masthead titles for multi-column pages easily in AppleWorks.

All you do is create a page with several sections. The masthead goes in the top section which is one column wide (extending from the left margin to the right margin); and the columns go in a second section that has multiple columns (see Figure 4.42).

To set a masthead:

1. Type the masthead text, then press Return.

2. Choose Insert Section Break from the Format menu. A section break appears in the document.

3. Choose Section from the Format menu.

4. In the Section dialog box, select the Start Section pop-up list and change the start of this section to New Line.

5. Change the number of columns in the box on the right side of the page to the number of columns you want to use.

6. Make appropriate changes for column width and space between columns.

7. Click the OK button when you are done.

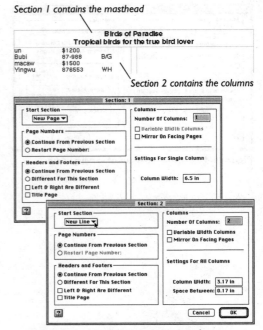

Section 1 contains the masthead

Section 2 contains the columns

Figure 4.42 A section can begin a new line, a new page, or a particular page—such as the left page or the right page. In this example, Section 1 begins a new page and Section 2 begins a new line.

ADVANCED WORD PROCESSING

Now that the basics are out of the way, let's investigate more advanced tools. This chapter teaches you about:

- Libraries and clip art
- Stylesheets
- Outlines
- Mail merge
- Macros

Libraries and clip art

You can find clip art collections via the Libraries... command on the File menu. This clip art may be used in conjunction with word processing, databases, or spreadsheets, and may be made any size.

Importing clip art

1. Click the location in the document where you want to place your clip art.

2. Choose Library from the File menu. The Library submenu appears (see Figure 5.1).

3. Select a library from the Library submenu. A library palette appears (see Figure 5.2).

4. Scroll down the picture list until you see a picture you want to use.

5. Click the Use button in the library palette.

or

Drag the picture from the library palette into your document.

6. To close the library palette, choose Close from its File menu.

You may import as many pictures into your document as you want—the only limitation is how much free disk space and free RAM your computer has.

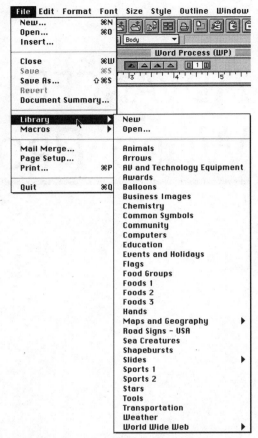

Figure 5.1 The Library submenu under the File menu.

Figure 5.2 Selecting an image from the Animals library palette.

ecumenical and bright ideas which seem impossible to
the vast luddite population that opposed the normal eve

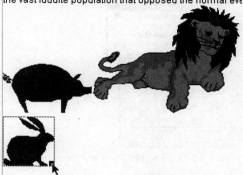

Figure 5.3 Inline graphics appear surrounded by a faint
gray line and have a small square dot on the lower-left
corner. Drag this dot to resize the graphic.

Figure 5.4 Poor bunny. When he was resized the Shift
key didn't get held down, so he is taller, but he is
narrower than he should be.

Resizing a picture

Pictures are easy to resize. To resize the picture you've imported:

1. Click anywhere in the picture to select it.

2. Click on the little black dot at the lower right corner of the picture (see Figures 5.3 and 5.4).

3. Hold the Shift key down.

4. Drag the picture corner dot at a 45° angle either up to make the picture smaller or down to make the picture larger.

5. Let go of the mouse button when the picture is the correct size.

If you don't hold down the shift key you will distort the picture.

Moving inline graphics

Inline graphics appear in the middle of a line of type, in a masthead, etc. Moving inline graphics is just like moving words.

To move an inline graphic:

1. Click the inline graphic you want to move.

2. Choose Cut from the Edit menu, or press ⌘-X on the Macintosh, or Control+X on Windows 95. The picture disappears.

3. Click where you want to place the picture.

4. Choose Paste from the Edit menu, or press ⌘-V on the Macintosh, or Control+V on Windows 95. The picture appears in the new position.

Library palette view options

You can view a library palette by name or by object. To change the view:

1. In the library palette, choose By Object from the View menu in the library palette. The pictures appear instead of the names (see Figure 5.5).

2. Choose By Name from the View menu in the library palette to see a list of image names.

3. Choose Alphabetize to alphabetize the name list of the clip art.

4. Choose View Options in the library palette to change the preview size of the pictures (see Figure 5.6).

Deleting a picture from a library

To delete a picture from a library palette, click on it and select Cut from the library palette's Edit menu.

Copying a picture in a library

Pictures in a library palette may be copied and pasted just like text in a document. To copy a picture, just click on it and select Copy from the Edit menu.

✔ Tips

■ You can alter clip art using photo-manipulation programs such as Adobe Photoshop.

■ You may use AppleWorks clip art without violating any copyright.

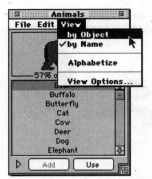

Figure 5.5 Choosing By Object in a library palette.

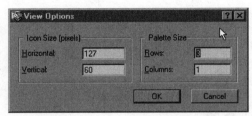

Figure 5.6 The library palette View Options dialog box.

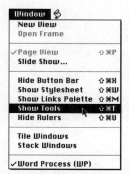

Figure 5.7 Choosing Show Tools under the Window menu.

Figure 5.8 Selecting the pointer tool (top left).

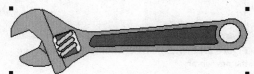

Figure 5.9 Freestanding graphics are surrounded by four square dots when they are selected. The pointer must be placed in the middle of the graphic before you move the graphic.

Creating freestanding graphics

Clip art may be placed as either an inline or a freestanding graphic. Freestanding graphics are graphics that may be freely moved around the page. If you click in a page before you open the libraries, you are creating inline graphics. Inline graphics are anchored to the location that you clicked. If you want to move your graphics around the page you must use freestanding graphics.

To create freestanding graphics:

1. Choose Show Tools from the Window menu, or press Shift-⌘-T on the Macintosh, or Shift+Control+T on Windows 95. The Tool palette appears (see Figure 5.7).

2. Choose the pointer tool on the Tool palette (see Figure 5.8).

3. Open the library you want to use and select the appropriate picture.

4. Click the Use button. The picture appears with a black dot on each corner of the picture area. This is a cue that the picture is a freestanding graphic and that you can move it (see Figure 5.9).

5. Click the close box to close the library.

Moving freestanding graphics

To move a freestanding graphic:

1. Choose Show Tools from the Windows menu, or press Shift-⌘-T on a Macintosh, or press Shift+Control+T on a Windows 95 machine.

2. Select the pointer tool from the Tool palette.

3. Click the center of the picture you want to move. Corner dots appear (see Figure 5.9).

4. Position the mouse pointer in the middle of the picture, hold the mouse button down, and drag the picture to the proper position.

Creating a new library

If you want to use your own collections of clip art in AppleWorks, you may create a library for them.

1. In any program, open a picture you want to add to the library. Choose Copy from the Edit menu.

2. In AppleWorks, choose Library from the File menu.

3. Select New from the Library submenu. An empty library palette appears (see Figure 5.10),

4. Choose Paste from the library palette's Edit menu. The inserted picture appears in the new library (see Figure 5.11).

5. Choose Save from the library palette's File menu (see Figure 5.12). The Save dialog box appears.

6. Type a name for this library in the name box.

7. Click the Save when you are done.

Figure 5.10 A new library.

Figure 5.11 Pasting an image from the clipboard into the new library.

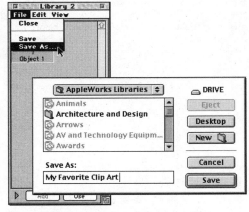

Figure 5.12 Saving (and naming) the new library.

MOVING FREESTANDING GRAPHICS

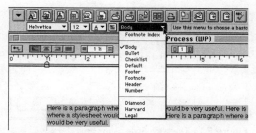

Figure 5.13 The Stylesheet pop-up menu on the Button bar.

Figure 5.14 The Stylesheet palette.

Stylesheets

Stylesheets are collections of information about text appearance. They can include many things beyond Bold, Italic, and Underline character styling. For example, stylesheets can also include text size, indents, whether or not bullets are used, etc. Stylesheets make formatting text much faster.

Stylesheet types

There are four basic stylesheet types:

- **Basic**—Text styles that apply to any highlighted character

- **Paragraph**—Text styles that apply to an entire paragraph, whether or not the entire paragraph is highlighted.

- **Outline**—Text styles that help you create an outline document.

- **Table**—Text styles for tables or imported spreadsheets.

Using stylesheets

1. Click in the paragraph to which you want to apply a stylesheet.

2. Choose a stylesheet from the stylesheets pop-up menu on the ruler bar (see Figure 5.13).

To use styles from the Window menu:

1. Click in the paragraph to which you want to apply a stylesheet.

2. Choose Show Stylesheets from the Window menu, or press Shift-⌘ -W on the Macintosh, or Shift+Control+W on Windows 95. The Stylesheet palette appears (see Figure 5.14).

3. Select the style you want to use from the Stylesheet palette.

STYLESHEETS

Creating a new style

You can use the Stylesheets palette to create new styles.

1. Format a paragraph of text to your satisfaction.

2. Highlight that paragraph.

3. Open the Stylesheets palette (press Shift-⌘ -W on the Macintosh, or Shift+Control+W on Windows 95).

4. Click the New button at the bottom of the Stylesheets Palette. The New Style dialog box appears (see Figure 5.15)

5. Type a name for the style in the Style Name box.

6. Click the appropriate button for the style type.

7. Click the Inherit Document selection format checkbox (Inherit checkbox).

8. Choose Default from the Based on pop-up menu.

9. Click the OK button when you are done.

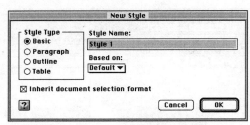

Figure 5.15 The New Style dialog box.

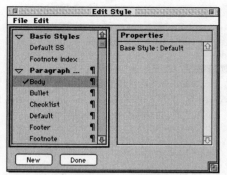

Figure 5.16 The Properties pane in the Stylesheet palette.

Figure 5.17 Copying a Property.

Editing stylesheets

You can edit stylesheets by viewing a list of properties (or characteristics), then cutting, copying and pasting the characteristics between stylesheets.

To edit a stylesheet:

1. Open the Stylesheets palette (press Shift-⌘-W on the Macintosh, or Shift+Control+W on Windows 95).

2. Click Edit at the bottom of the Stylesheets Palette. The Properties list appears.

3. Click the stylesheet you want to edit. The properties for that stylesheet appear in the Properties list (see Figure 5.16).

4. Click any property you want to delete. Choose Cut Property from the palette's Edit menu. The property disappears from the Properties list.

5. Click any property you want to borrow for another style. Choose Copy Property from the palette's Edit list (see Figure 5.17).

6. Click the stylesheet that you want to move this property into and click in the Properties pane. Choose Paste Property from the palette's Edit menu.

7. Click any property you want to permanently delete from a stylesheet. Choose Clear Property from the palette's Edit menu. The property is permanently deleted.

Label

Label is a third way of using stylesheets. Remember that the other two ways are using the Stylesheets pop-up menu on the Button bar and using Show Stylesheets from the Window menu.

To use Label:

1. Highlight the paragraph you want to change. You may also select more than one paragraph, or use Select All from the Edit menu to select the entire document.

2. Choose Paragraph from the Format menu. The Paragraph dialog box appears.

3. Choose the style you want to use from the Label pop-up list in the Paragraph dialog box. (See Figure 5.18).

4. Click the OK button when you are done.

Importing styles

If you have a perfect set of styles in another document, you may import them into your current document and use them.

To import styles:

1. Open the Stylesheet palette (press Shift-⌘-W on the Macintosh, or Shift+Control+W on Windows 95).

2. Select Import Styles from the File menu (see Figure 5.19). An Open dialog box appears.

3. Select the document that contains the styles you want to import and press the Open button. A list of styles appears in the Selected Styles to Import dialog box (see Figure 5.20)

4. Check the styles you wish to import.

5. Click the OK button when you are finished. The imported styles appear in the Stylesheet palette.

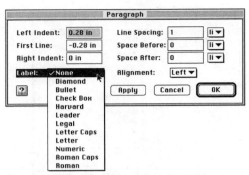

Figure 5.18 The Label pop-up list in the Paragraph dialog box.

Figure 5.19 Import styles using the File menu in rhe Stylesheet palette.

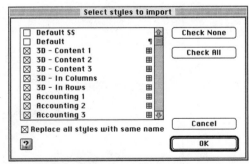

Figure 5.20 The Select Styles to Import dialog box.

STYLESHEETS

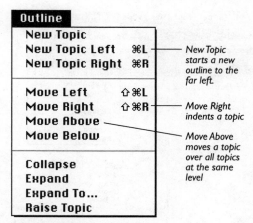

Figure 5.21 The Outline menu.

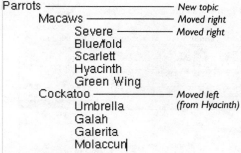

Figure 5.22 Typing an outline.

Outlines

Outlines let you build documents based on logic. Think of a table of contents as an outline. Each entry has text attached to it. Outlines give you topics and sub-topics to work with when preparing an important document.

Creating an outline

To create an outline:

1. Click on a new line or create a new line by pressing the Return key.

2. Choose New Topic from the Outline menu (see Figure 5.21).

3. Type the information for your first major point, even if that information takes more than one line.

4. Press the Return key. Your typing cursor is now in position for you to begin typing the next major point.

Sub-topics

Sub-topics are indented points of the outline that fall under the main new topic points. To create a sub-topic:

1. Create the main topic as shown above.

2. Press the Return key to create a new blank line.

3. Choose New Topic Right from the Outline menu, or press ⌘-R if you are on a Macintosh, or Control+R for Windows 95. The cursor appears to be indented. Begin typing your sub-topic (see Figure 5.22).

4. Press the Return key when you are finished. The cursor returns to the same level as the current sub-topic.

OUTLINES

Returning to a previous level

Once you indent a topic using New Topic Right, you must return to the main topic level when you are finished. To return to the previous topic level:

1. After typing the sub-topic, press the Return key.

2. Choose New Topic Left from the Outline menu, or press ⌘-L on the Macintosh, or Control+L on Windows 95. The cursor moves back to the left.

Changing topic levels

If you want to change your outline so that a major point becomes a sub-topic, or a sub-topic become a major topic, you need to move a topic (see Figure 5.23).

To move topics:

1. Click anywhere inside of the topic you want to change.

2. Choose Move Right on the Outline menu (Shift-⌘-R on the Macintosh, Shift+Control+R on Windows 95) to indent the topic;

or

Choose Move Left on the Outline menu (Shift-⌘-L on the Macintosh, Shift+Control+L on Windows 95) to remove a level.

Changing topic order

To move a topic above another topic:

1. Click on the topic you want to move.

2. Select Move Above from the Outline menu (see Figure 5.24).

Moving a topic below another topic works exactly the same way.

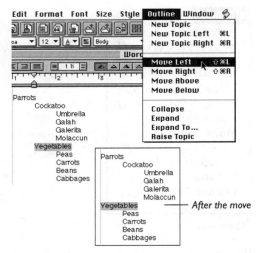

Figure 5.23 Moving a topic left.

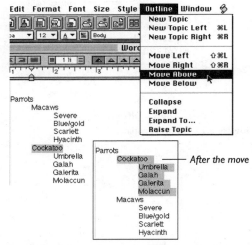

Figure 5.24 Moving a topic above. Click on Cockatoo, then press Move Above on the Outline menu. The Cockatoo topic and subtopics associated with it move above previous topics on the same level.

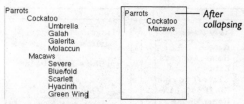

Figure 5.25 This example shows the full outline collapsed to two main topics: Cockatoo and Macaws. The subitems are still there, they are just hidden from view.

Collapsing and expanding topics

Collapsing and expanding topics means you can collapse a topic so that you only see the main points, but the sub-topics are still there—they are just hidden from view. Expanding topics means you can make the temporarily hidden sub-topics visible (see Figure 5.25).

To collapse or expand an outline:

1. Highlight your outline or the portions of it you want to collapse or expand.

2. Choose Collapse or Expand from the Outline menu.

You do not need to see all levels of sub-topics when you partially expand an outline:

1. Click on the topic you want to partially expand.

2. Select Expand To from the Outline menu. The Expand dialog box appears.

3. Type the number of levels you want to see in the Expand dialog box.

4. Click the OK button when you are done.

Mail Merge

In order to use Mail Merge, you must first create a database. See Chapter 7, "Database," to learn how to create a simple database for use with Mail Merge.

If you already know how to create a database or if you have your information in a AppleWorks database, then:

1. Open a blank word processing document.

2. Type the letter or other document to be merged, leaving out all of the information that is in the database. Usually this information consists of names, addresses, city, states, and Zip codes.

3. Choose Mail Merge from the File menu. The Open dialog box appears.

4. Select the database that contains the information you want to insert into your mail merge. The Mail Merge palette appears (see Figure 5.26).

5. Insert the fields from the database into the appropriate position in the mail merge file (see Figure 5.27).

6. Click the Print Merge button when you are finished.

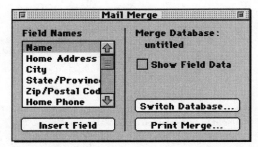

Figure 5.26 The Mail Merge palette shows a list of all fields you can use in your database.

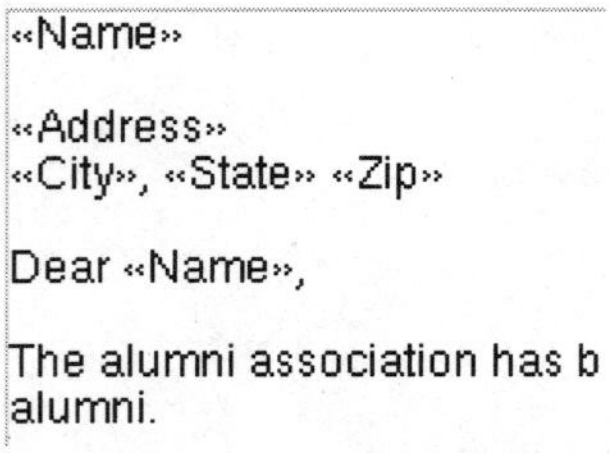

«Name»

«Address»
«City», «State» «Zip»

Dear «Name»,

The alumni association has b alumni.

Figure 5.27 As fields are entered into the document, they appear with brackets around them: <<Name>>. Later when the merge is performed, instead of seeing <<Name>> the actual information in the name field appears.

Inserting fields into a merge document

To insert a field:

1. With the Mail Merge palette open, click where you want the field to appear.

2. Select the field you want to use from the Field list in the Mail Merge dialog box.

3. Click the Insert Field button. The field appears in the document.

4. Repeat steps 1 through 3 until you have inserted all the fields you need.

✔ Tips

- You do not need to use all fields from the database.

- You may use a field from a database more than once.

- To see the information inserted into the document instead of just the field name, select the Show Field Data box in the Mail Merge dialog box.

- Double-check the placement of all database fields within your document.

- You can use mail merge when printing onto any type of paper, including mailing labels and envelopes.

- Click the Switch Database button to use a different database for a document. It's best to use only one database per document. If you switch from one database to another while inserting fields, the field entries from the first database may not print.

MAIL MERGE

Macros

Macros save time by recording and automating the steps of a process for later re-use. You can use macros to type text, make menu selections, open documents—anything you can do with AppleWorks can become a macro.

Creating a macro

1. Choose Macros from the File menu. The Macros sub-menu appears.

2. Select Record Macro from the Macros submenu, or press Shift-⌘-J on the Macintosh, or Shift+Control+J on Windows 95. The Record Macro dialog box appears (see Figure 5.28).

3. Type a short name for the macro in the name box of the Record Macro dialog box.

4. Type a key combination for your macro. You may either use one of the function keys at the top of the keyboard, or a combination of the ⌘ and Option keys plus another key on the Macintosh (for example, ⌘-Option-T), or Control and Alt plus another key on Windows 95 (for example, Control+Alt+U).

5. Select the type of documents you want your macro to work with from the Play In pane of the Macros dialog box.

6. Click the Record button.

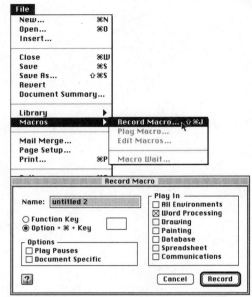

Figure 5.28 Recording a macro and the Record Macro dialog box.

Figure 5.29 Stopping recording the macro.

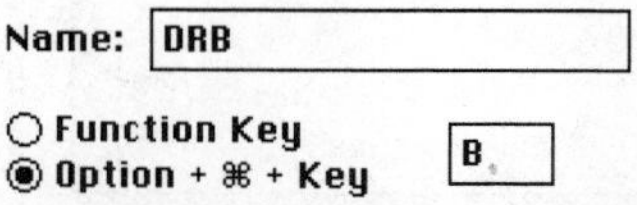

Name: DRB

○ **Function Key**
◉ **Option + ⌘ + Key** B

Figure 5.30 Try to use a letter key that reminds you of what that macro does. For example, "N" could be a macro that types your name. Control+Alt+key on Windows 95 is ⌘-Option-key on the Macintosh.

7. Perform all of the actions and typing you want the macro to remember. If you make mistakes, just do what you normally would do to fix those mistakes. Later, when you play the macro back, the macro will first make those same mistakes, then it will do what you did to correct those mistakes—but it performs the actions so fast that you will only see the final results.

8. Choose Stop Recording from the Macros sub-menu under the File menu, or press Shift-⌘-J on the Macintosh, or Shift+Control+J on Windows 95. The macro stops recording (see Figure 5.29).

Assigning a shortcut key

1. Perform all of the steps in "Creating a macro" above.

2. With the Record macro dialog box open, find the radio buttons for keys to be used with a macro (see Figure 5.30).

3. Click either the Function key choice or the Control+Alt+key choice.

4. If you have selected the Function key radio button, tap the Function key you want to use.

5. If you have selected the ⌘+Option+key or Control+Alt+key, type a letter to be used with the Control and Alt keys in the square box on the right side of the radio button.

MACROS

Playing a macro

There are two ways to play a macro:

- Use Play Macro from the Macros sub-menu of the File menu.

- Use the shortcut key you assigned to the macro.

To play a macro using Play Macro:

1. Select Macros from the File menu. The Macros sub-menu appears.

2. Select Play macro from the Macros sub-menu on the File menu. The Play Macro dialog box appears (See Figure 5.31).

3. Select the macro you want to play from the macro list in the Play Macro dialog box.

4. Click the Play button. The macro plays.

To play a macro using shortcut keys:

Press the shortcut key combination you assigned to the macro.

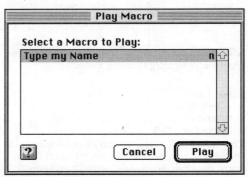

Figure 5.31 The Play Macro dialog box.

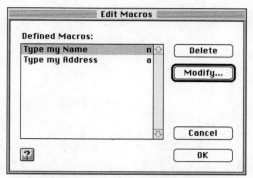

Figure 5.32 The Edit Macros dialog box displays a list of all available macros.

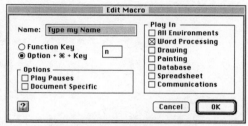

Figure 5.33 The Edit Macro dialog box.

Editing a macro

Editing a macro is limited to editing the choices you made in the Edit Macro dialog box. You can change the shortcut key or the environments in which you want to play the macro. If you need to change what the macro does, you need to delete the macro and re-record it.

To edit a macro:

1. Select Macros from the File menu. The Macros sub-menu appears.

2. Select Edit from the Macros sub-menu on the File menu. The Edit Macros dialog box appears (see Figure 5.32).

3. Select the macro you want to edit from the Macros list in the Edit Macros dialog box.

4. Click the Modify button in the Edit dialog box. The Edit Macro dialog box appears.

5. Make any changes you desire in the Edit Macro dialog box (see Figure 5.33).

✔ Tip

■ If you don't remember the shortcut key you assigned to a macro, try editing the macro. When the Edit dialog box appears, the shortcut key combination appears on the right side of the macro list. Click the Cancel button to return to the document.

MACROS

BEGINNING SPREADSHEETS

Spreadsheets are great for figuring out budgets or calculating revenue streams. Spreadsheets are made up of:

- **Rows**—extend from right to left and are numbered beginning with the number 1.
- **Columns**—extend from top to bottom and are lettered from left to right, beginning with the letter A, going to Z, then starting up again with AA.
- **Cells**—the intersection between a row and a column. Cells are named by first their column designation, followed by the cell designation. For example, cell A1.

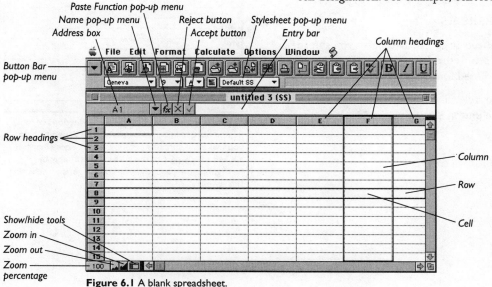

Figure 6.1 A blank spreadsheet.

A spreadsheet is like a piece of ledger paper, with rows ranging from 1 to 500 and columns from column A to AN. When you print a very large spreadsheet, AppleWorks makes logically sized paper pages out of the large electronic page.

The very last cell of a AppleWorks spreadsheet is cell AN500 (see Figure 6.2). Although you have all of that space, it is not a good idea to fill all of the cells as the spreadsheet may load slowly, or not at all. If the project is going to be very large, use a database instead of a spreadsheet. While databases are not the same as spreadsheets, they use the same mathematical functions, and you can use them as if they were spreadsheets.

Spreadsheet tools

There are many tools in the spreadsheet module that help you enter your data more efficiently and help you make your spreadsheet more beautiful. Among these tools are pop-up menus for giving areas of the spreadsheet a name, for pasting functions, a toolbox, and buttons for accepting or rejecting entered data (see Figure 6.3).

Stylesheets

Stylesheets in spreadsheets give you spreadsheet setups that have different backgrounds and colored fonts.

To use style sheets, click the stylesheet button on the Button Bar (See Figure 6.4).

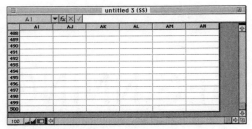

Figure 6.2 The very last cell of the spreadsheet.

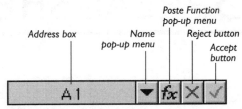

Figure 6.3 Spreadsheet tools.

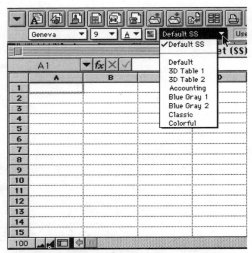

Figure 6.4 Stylesheets are preset collections of font, fill, and border information that are designed to help you make the spreadsheet look better. Styles may be applied to any part of the spreadsheet simply by highlighting the part you wish to change, then selecting the style.

Name pop-up menu

The Name pop-up menu gives you commands that help you assign a name to any
area of a spreadsheet. You may use the name
instead of the cell addresses in functions.
Also, when names are assigned, instead of
seeing the cell address (for example A1) in
the cell address box, you see the cell name.

Paste Function pop-up menu

The Paste Function pop-up menu gives you a
dialog box containing all of the functions you
may use in AppleWorks spreadsheets.
Functions are predefined mathematical operations that help you calculate complicated
math such as

- Business and Financial functions
- Date and Time functions
- Informational functions
- Logical functions
- Numeric functions
- Statistical functions
- Text functions
- Trigonometric functions

Accept and Reject buttons

You may enter data by typing it, then pressing
the Return key. You may also enter data by
clicking the Accept button on the data entry
bar. If you type information that is incorrect,
click the Reject button on the data entry bar.

Additional tools

Two other tools are useful when using spreadsheets: the Toolbox and Button Bar pop-up menu.

Toolbox

The toolbox (see Figure 6.5) helps you draw shapes or lines, place color into shapes, and paint within your spreadsheet. You access the toolbox by clicking on the Toolbox button at the bottom of the spreadsheet.

Button Bar pop-up menu

You may use the Button Bar pop-up menu (see Figure 6.6) to help you choose other Button Bars with additional functions. Additional Button Bars include:

- Internet
- Assistant
- Default
- Document

When you select a new toolbar from the Button Bar pop-up menu, the default toolbar disappears and is replaced by the new toolbar.

To change toolbars using the Button Bar:

1. Click the Button Bar pop-up menu button. The pop-up menu appears.

2. Select the Button Bar menu you want to use. The new Button Bar appears and the default Button Bar disappears.

To change back to the default Button Bar follow the same steps but select the default Button Bar.

Figure 6.5 The spreadsheet toolbox contains the same tools found in word processing, database, drawing, and painting.

Figure 6.6 The Button Bar pop-up menu lists all of the toolbars that may be used in spreadsheets.

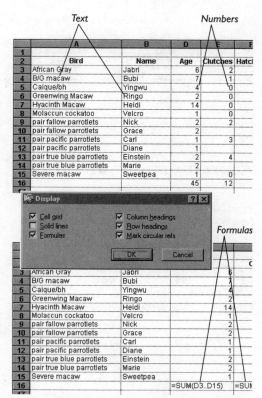

Figure 6.7 Functions in spreadsheets can be made visible by choosing Display from the Options menu and selecting Formulas in the Options dialog box.

Table 6.1

Moving Around the Spreadsheet	
MOVEMENT	KEY
Moving to Home (A1)	Home key
Moving to last cell (AN500)	End
Move forward a cell	Tab
Move backward a cell	Shift + Tab
Down one screenful	Page down

Spreadsheet data

You may enter three types of information into any spreadsheet:

- **Text**—Text is normally left-aligned within a cell. You may reformat the text so that it is centered or right-aligned.

- **Numbers**—Numbers are normally right-justified. Numbers are also entered without the ".00" for even dollar amounts. Trailing zeroes are filled in later when numbers are formatted.

- **Functions**—Totals for columns, averages, and any type of math are figured out by using functions. Functions always refer to the location of the cell. For example: = sum(A1+A2) which adds up the contents of cell A1 and cell A2 (see Figure 6.7).

Text is typed in "as desired," meaning you type the text in as you want it to appear, with capital letters, hyphens, and punctuation.

Numbers are typed in, but are formatted later. If you want a dollar sign to appear before a number just typed in the number. Add the dollar sign later with the format command.

Moving around

You need easy ways to move in spreadsheets. You may use the mouse to click any cell you want to enter information into, but it is easier to move if you use one of the ways in Table 6.1.

Starting a spreadsheet

Entering information

You enter data in the data entry box, not directly into the spreadsheet.

To begin entering data:

1. Select New from the File menu.

2. Select Spreadsheet from the opening dialog box.

3. Click the OK button. The blank spreadsheet appears.

4. Click the cell in which you want to place information.

5. Type the information you want to place in that cell. The information appears in the data entry box at the top of the spreadsheet (see Figure 6.8)

6. Press the Enter key to enter the information into the spreadsheet.

Changing information

Once you have entered information into the spreadsheet, you may need to edit it.

To edit information, click the cell containing the incorrect information. Type the correct information and press the Return key when you are done. Or …

1. Click the cell that contains the incorrect information.

2. Then click the data entry box at the top of the spreadsheet and edit your text there (see Figure 6.9).

3. Press the Return key when you are finished.

The active cell will contain the information

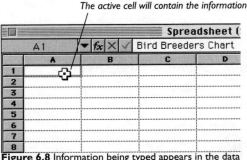

Figure 6.8 Information being typed appears in the data entry area.

Click here to begin editing.   *Actual editing takes place here.*

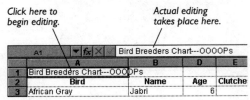

Figure 6.9 Changing information in a cell.

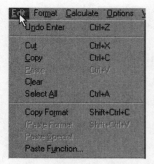

Figure 6.10 Cut from the Edit menu and Clear both erase text, but Clear makes sure you cannot recover the information.

Removing information

You may erase information from a cell in several ways. Click the cell containing the information you want to erase and perform one of the following procedures:

- Press the Clear or Delete key.

- Select Cut from the Edit menu. If you use Cut, you are able to paste the information somewhere else in the spreadsheet (see Figure 6.10). If you select Clear, the information is absolutely gone and you will not be able to paste it anywhere.

STARTING A SPREADSHEET

Resizing rows and columns

Rows and columns appear in a default height and width. This size may not be correct for the project you are creating.

When you type text in a cell and the text is longer than the cell is wide, it may appear to spill over into the next cell—if that cell is empty. However, if you go on to enter data into the empty cell, you will not be able to see all of the information in the first cell.

You should always make columns just as wide as you need them to be to hold the widest entry in the column, but no wider.

Resizing columns

To change a column's width:

1. Move the mouse pointer to the line between the column heading of the column you want to widen and the one to the right of it (see Figure 6.11).
   The pointer should appear as a double-headed arrow. If does not, you need to move the pointer until it is exactly over the line.

2. Hold the mouse button down and drag the double-headed arrow right (to widen) or left (to narrow the column).

3. When the column is the correct width, let go of the mouse button.

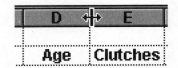

Figure 6.11 Changing a column's width.

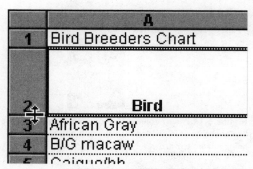

Figure 6.12 This row is resized so that it is taller. This is necessary if you are going to use larger type sizes.

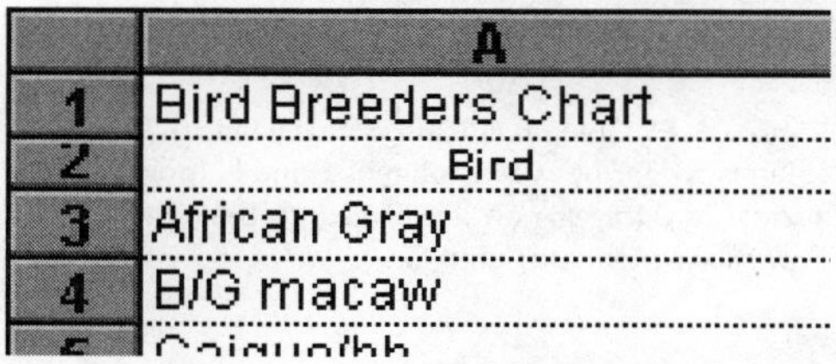

	A
1	Bird Breeders Chart
2	Bird
3	African Gray
4	B/G macaw
5	Caique/bb

Figure 6.13 Row 2 is very short. The data in Row 2 is only 9 points tall.

Resizing rows

Rows are only one line high, but if you want to use much larger text, you might need more height.

To make a row taller:

1. Move the mouse pointer to the line just below a row heading on the left-hand side of the spreadsheet. The pointer should appear as a double-headed arrow.

2. Hold the mouse button down and drag the line down until the line is as tall as you want it to be (see Figure 6.12).

To make a row shorter:

1. Move the cursor to the line that appears just below the row number on the left-hand side of the spreadsheet.

2. Hold the mouse button down and drag the line up until the line is as short as you want it to be (see Figure 6.13).

RESIZING ROWS AND COLUMNS

Hiding columns or rows

If you want to add data but don't want every-one to see some of it, you may hide a column or a row (See Figure 6.15 and 6.16).

To hide a column or row:

1. Move the mouse pointer to the column or row divider (just as you would to make the column narrow or to resize the row).

2. Hold the mouse button down and drag the column divider to the left until the column disappears, or drag the row divider down until the row disappears (see Figure 6.14).

3. The column or row is hidden (see Figure 6.15).

If you hide a column or row, later you might need to see the information.

To restore a hidden column or row to view:

1. Move the pointer to the column or row divider where the column or row is missing.

2. Drag the divider to the right for a column, or down for a row.

3. Let go of the mouse button when you are finished.

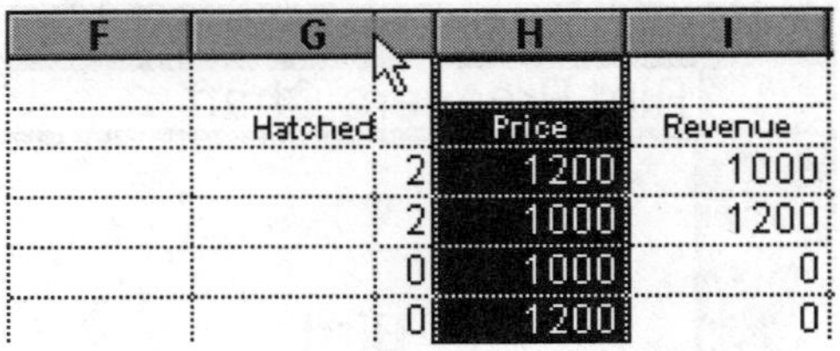

Figure 6.14 Hiding column G. Notice the faint gray line as the column divider between columns G and H is being moved toward column F.

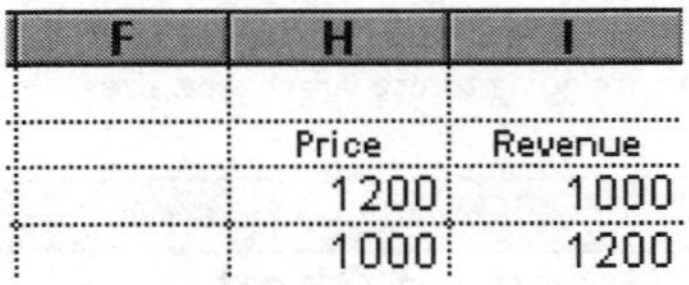

Figure 6.15 Column G is now totally hidden. The column divider between columns F and H looks normal, but dragging on this divider to the right will expose the hidden column G.

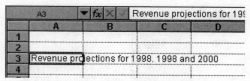

Figure 6.16 This line is too long to fit in cell A3. It appears to extend into columns B, C, and D.

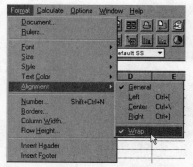

Figure 6.17 Select Wrap on the Alignment choice from the Format menu.

Figure 6.18 The line was collapsed into one cell using Wrap. To make the text visible, the row was then made taller.

Wrapping text

If you can't make a column wide enough to contain information, or if you have more than one line of information, such as a paragraph of text, you may word-wrap the text within a cell.

To word-wrap text in a spreadsheet:

1. Type the text in the cell you want to use, even if the text is very long (see Figure 6.16).

2. Click the cell containing the text.

3. Select Wrap from the Alignment submenu on the Format menu (see Figure 6.17).

4. Resize the row to the proper height until all of the text appears (see Figure 6.18).

Adding rows or columns

After laying out a spreadsheet, you might need to add a row or a column in the middle of your layout. When you add columns, the new column is inserted to the left of the selected column. New rows are always inserted above the selected row.

To add a row or column:

1. Click on a row header number or a column header letter. The row or column is selected (see Figure 6.19).

2. Select Insert Cells from the Calculate menu (press Shift-⌘-I on the Macintosh or Shift+Control+I on Windows 95). The new row or column appears (see Figures 6.20 and 6.21).

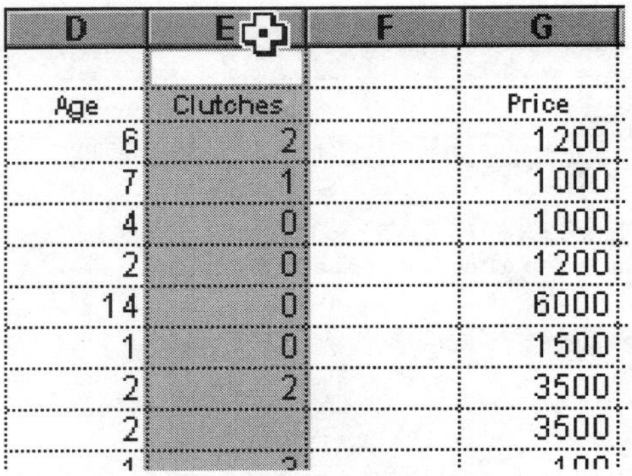

Deleting rows or columns

Deleting rows or columns is almost the same as adding them.

To delete rows:

1. Click on a row header number or a column header letter. The row or column is selected.

2. Select Delete Cells from the Calculate menu (Shift-⌘-K on the Macintosh or Shift+Control+K on Windows 95). The row or column disappears.

Figure 6.19 Selecting a column.

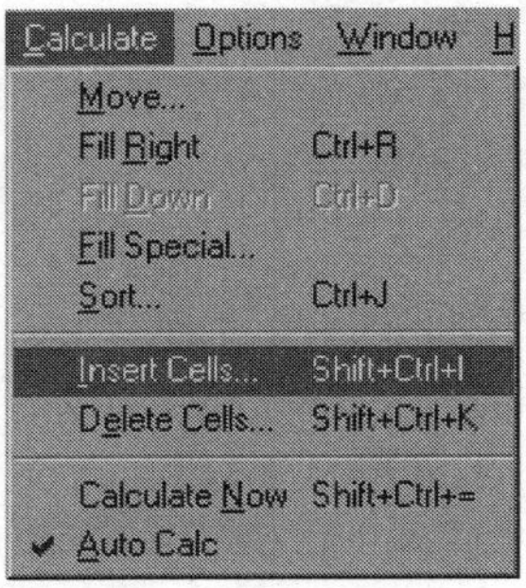

Figure 6.20 Insert Cells and Delete Cells on the Calculate menu.

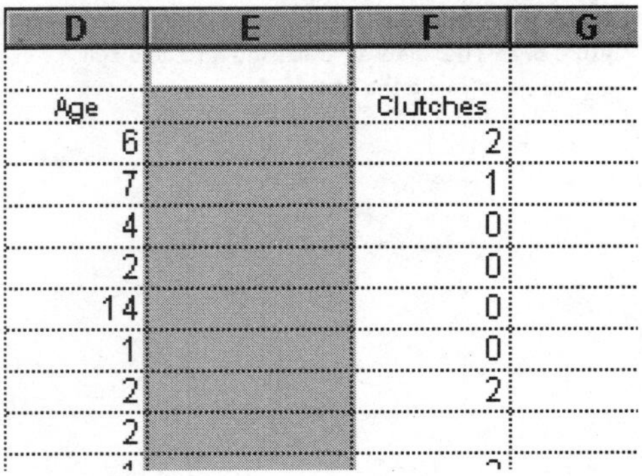

Figure 6.21 The spreadsheet after the column has been inserted.

Create a blank column first.

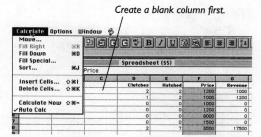

Figure 6.22 Moving column F to column C. The highlighted column is going to be moved.

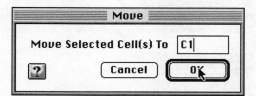

Figure 6.23 Entering the destination in the Move dialog box.

C	D	E	F	G
Price	Clutches	Hatched		Revenue
1200	2	2		1000
1000	1	2		1200
1000	0	0		0
1200	0	0		0
8000	0	0		0
1500	0	0		0
3500	2	7		17500

Figure 6.24 After the move.

Moving columns and rows

Need to swap things around? Moving can be a little tricky, so follow these instructions precisely.

To move a column or row:

1. Create a new row or column exactly where you want to move information. **Do not skip this step.** Otherwise, you will paste the information you want to move on top of other information you want to save.

2. Select the row or column you want to move (see Figure 6.22).

3. Select Move from the calculate menu. The Move dialog box appears (see Figure 6.23).

4. In the dialog box, type the cell address of the beginning of the new location for the information. Make sure you are moving the information to a completely empty column or row.

5. Click the OK button when you are done (see Figure 6.24).

MOVING COLUMNS AND ROWS

Copying and pasting data

Some information is useful in more than one location. You may copy and paste information from more than one cell at a time, or information from just one cell (see Figure 6.25). Information may be typed text, typed numbers, or functions. If you copy functions, only the function is copied, not the calculated results.

To copy and paste information:

1. Create a new row or column, if needed.

2. Select the information you want to copy by highlighting the row, column, range, or cell (see Figure 6.26).

3. Select Copy from the Edit menu (⌘-C on the Macintosh or Control+C on Windows 95). The information is copied invisibly to the clipboard. Now you are ready to paste it.

4. Click the first cell where you want to place your information (see Figure 6.27).

5. Select Paste from the Edit menu, or press ⌘-V on the Macintosh, or press Control+V if you are on Windows 95. The information appears (see Figure 6.28).

You may paste information from one spreadsheet to another, or you may paste information from spreadsheets into a AppleWorks word processing document. The steps are the same: Highlight the information, select Copy from the Edit menu, then select Paste.

You may also paste information from word processing into spreadsheets, or from any of the AppleWorks modules into spreadsheets, or into any of the other AppleWorks modules.

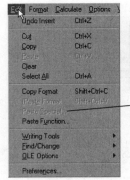

Use Paste Special when you want to paste the results of functions, but not the function itself. To paste just the results, select the Paste Values Only radio button in the Paste Special dialog box.

Figure 6.25 Cut, Copy, and Paste are always on the Edit menu in all modules of AppleWorks.

Figure 6.26 Highlight the cells to be copied.

Figure 6.27 The first cell where the data will appear (A17).

Figure 6.28 The information appears beginning in Cell A17.

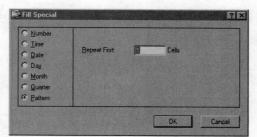

Figure 6.29 Details in the right side of the Fill Special dialog box vary depending on which Fill radio button is selected.

Automatic fill

Save time! Save work! Let AppleWorks fill in the cells for you. If you are using information that increases with each row or column, you can use automatic fill. For example, say you want each row to contain a date for each day of the week. You may use automatic fill with:

- Number
- Time
- Date
- Day
- Month
- Quarter
- Pattern (you set up the pattern you want)

To use automatic fill:

1. Highlight the range of cells you want to contain the automatic data.

2. Select Fill Special from the Calculate menu. The Fill Special dialog box appears (See Figure 6.29).

3. Click the radio button for the type of fill you want to use.

4. Click the OK button.

Details may be changed in the Fill pane of the Fill Special dialog box.

Fill pattern

Fill pattern allows you to repeat a selected group of cells.

To use Fill pattern:

1. Highlight the cells you want to use for the fill and the cells that you want to fill.

2. Select Fill Special from the Calculate menu. The Fill Special dialog box appears.

3. Click the Pattern radio button in the Fill Special dialog box.

4. Fill in how many cells you want to use for the fill in the Repeat cells box.

   For example, if the first four cells (A1 through A4) contain the information you want to use in cells A5 through A17, highlight cells A1 through A17. In the Repeat Cells dialog box, type the number 4, which tells Calculate to use cells A1 through A4.

5. Click the OK button when you are finished.

Fill down

Fill down lets you copy information in one cell to as many cells as are adjacent to that cell and that extend down.

To use Fill down:

1. Highlight both the cell that contains the information to be used as the fill and the blank cells where the information is to be filled (see Figure 6.30).

2. Select Fill Down from the Calculate menu. The cells are all filed with copies of the information that was in the first cell (See Figure 6.31).

3. Click the OK button when you are finished.

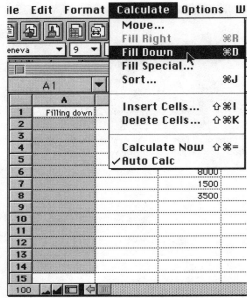

Figure 6.30 Before using Fill Down.

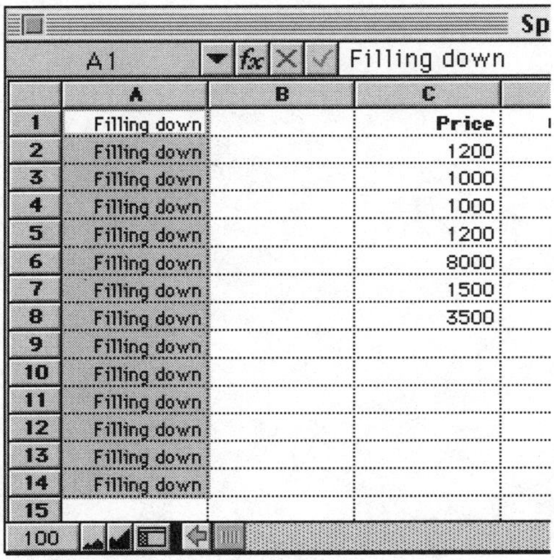

Figure 6.31 After using Fill Down.

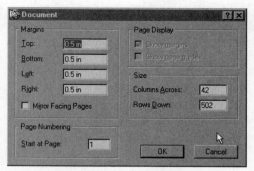

Figure 6.32 Format Document allows you to change margins, page numbers, and how many columns and rows you want the spreadsheet to contain.

Formatting spreadsheets

Document formatting

To change margins, page numbering, and overall size of spreadsheets:

1. Select document from the Format menu. The Document dialog box appears (see Figure 6.32).

2. Type the Top, Bottom, Left and Right margin measurements you want to use in the appropriate boxes.

3. Type the first page number you want the spreadsheet to use when you print it out in the Page number box.

4. Type the number of columns you want the spreadsheet to have in the Columns box of the Size pane.

5. Type the number of rows down you want the spreadsheet to have.

6. Click the OK button when you are finished.

Text formatting

Text formatting means applying attributes to text such as bold, underline, color, a new typeface, font size, or changing the alignment.

To use text formatting:

1. Select the cells that contain text you want to change.

2. Select one of the following options from the Format menu:
    —Font
    —Size
    —Style
    —Text Color
    —Alignment

3. Choose the options you want to use in the submenu that appears for the formatting choice.

FORMATTING SPREADSHEETS

Formatting numbers

When you type numbers in spreadsheets, type the number. Don't type in dollar signs, or commas—instead use the number formatting options.

To format numbers:

1. Select the cell, column, row, or range that you want to format.

2. Choose Number from the Format menu (Shift-⌘-N if you are on the Macintosh, or Shift+Control+N if you are on Windows 95).

3. Click the appropriate radio buttons in the Number, Date, or Time panes in the Format Number dialog box (see Figure 6.33).

4. If you select Currency or Number, you need to specify in the Precision box how many digits go after the decimal point.

5. Click the OK button when you are finished.

Ranges

A range is a generic way of referring to any area of the spreadsheet. For example from cell A1 to cell A15 is a range that contains 15 cells in column A. A range of A1 to Z1 includes 26 cells in row 1. A range from C1 to E8 includes all cells beginning in cell C1 to cell C8 and from cell E1 to E8. C1 is the upper left-hand corner of the range and cell E8 is the lower right-hand corner of the range (see Figure 6.34).

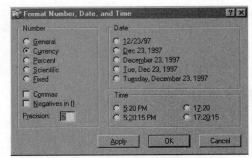

Figure 6.33 The Format Number dialog box.

	A	B	C	D	E
1			Price	Clutches	Hatched
2			1200	2	2
3			1000	1	2
4			1000	0	0
5			1200	0	0
6			8000	0	0
7			1500	0	0
8			3500	2	7
9					
10					

Figure 6.34 The range C1 to E8 is selected.

```
=SUM(I3..I15)
```

Figure 6.35 Formulas must be typed with no spaces between any letters, numbers, symbols, or characters.

Functions

Functions are math equations. They can easily add, subtract, calculate interest rates, determine cosines, and do lots of other things we all struggled with in school. Functions always refer to the location of the cell.

What distinguishes a function is the "=" sign at the beginning. The function "SUM" after the equal sign does not just mean add, it means perform any math that is indicated between the two parentheses that follow.

The basic function looks like this:

=SUM(math goes in here) or =SUM(A1+D25)

To use =SUM:

1. Click in the cell you want the answer to the function to be.

2. Type =SUM(

3. Type each cell reference plus the + or – to indicate addition or subtraction, or * or / to indicate multiply or divide (see Figure 6.35).

4. End the function with a right parenthesis.

It is time consuming to type a long range of cell addresses into a function (for instance A1+A2+A3+A4+A5). Instead, you can use the ranges in the function. The range for this last example is from cell A1 to and including cell A5, or more properly A1..A5. The function now reads =SUM(A1..A5).

Ranges and cell addresses may be typed in either upper or lower case.

Defining functions

To define the function in a cell:

1. Click in the cell where you want a function to appear.

2. Select Paste Function from the Edit menu. The Paste Function dialog box appears (see Figure 6.36).

3. Scroll through the list of functions to the function you want to use.

4. Select the function you want to use.

5. Click the OK button. You are returned to the spreadsheet.

Edit the function in the data entry area of the spreadsheet at the top, until the function contains all of the proper cells.

Copying and pasting functions

You can copy functions from one cell to another in a spreadsheet.

1. Highlight the cell or range that contains the function(s) you want to copy.

2. Select Copy from the edit menu.

3. Select the cell or range where you want to place the function.

4. Select Paste from the Edit menu. The function is pasted, and the cell references are changed relative to the new position.

The IF function

The spreadsheet has pre-built functions that are set up for you to use. We have shown you how to use =SUM, which is the simplest one. IF is a slightly more complicated function.

IF is a wonderful function that lets you have two possibilities for an answer. If the IF function was running your home, it might give

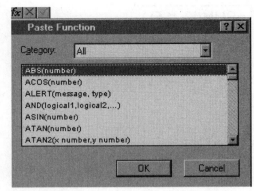

Figure 6.36 You may either type a function directly into the spreadsheet, or choose the formula from the Paste Function pop-up button. Click the formula in the formula list, then click the OK button.

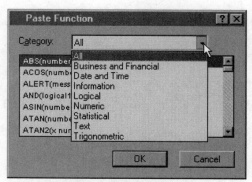

Figure 6.37 The Paste Function dialog box.

=IF(logical,true value,false value)

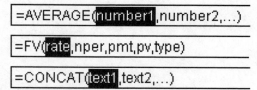

Figure 6.38 The IF function in the spreadsheet's Entry bar.

=AVERAGE(number1,number2,...)

=FV(rate,nper,pmt,pv,type)

=CONCAT(text1,text2,...)

Figure 6.39 Once formulas are entered from the Paste Function dialog box, highlight the textual cues and enter the appropriate cellular reference.

your kids two choices: If you don't eat your peas, you will go to bed early, otherwise if you do eat your peas you may have ice cream for dessert.

Here is how you set up the IF function:

1. Click in the cell where you want the results of the function to be displayed.
2. Choose Paste Function from the Edit menu. The Paste Function dialog box appears (see Figure 6.37).
3. Scroll down the list in the Function dialog box until you see IF(logical,true value,false value).
4. When you see the IF function in the Function dialog box, select the function.
5. Click the OK button. The IF function appears in the data entry area.
6. Select the phrase "logical" in the IF function in the data entry area and enter in what you want for the function to evaluate (see Figures 6.38 and 6.39).
7. Select the phrase "false-value" and enter what you want the function to display if the cell it looks at does not equal what it is evaluating.
8. Select the phrase "true-value" and enter what you want the function to display if the cell it looks at equals what it is evaluating.
9. Click the Return key to enter the function.

✔ Tip

- A quick way to get to the IF function is type an "I" when you see the Paste Function dialog box.

Options

Options allow you to make universal changes to the spreadsheet such as:

- Locking cells to prevent data entry into those cells

- Adding page breaks so the spreadsheet will print the way you want it to print

- Locking the Title position which allows you to freeze as many rows as you like at the top so that they are always in view as you scroll further down the spreadsheet

- Set Print Range which tells the printer exactly which range of cells to print

- Default Font which allows you to set the normal font for the spreadsheet. This option is something you should choose before you start creating the spreadsheet.

- Display which sets what you would like to see on the screen including column and row labels, grid lines, or functions instead of the results in cells.

The Options menu (see Figure 6.40) also contains a useful shortcut, Go To Cell, which is used to move you quickly to any cell that you for which you know the address. Use Go To Cell by pressing ⌘-G on the Macintosh, or Control+G on Windows 95.

To use options:

1. Choose the option you want from the Options menu.

2. Select the radio buttons, fonts, or range of cells to which you want the option to apply.

3. Click the OK button when you are finished.

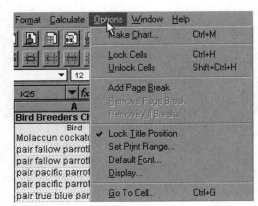

Figure 6.40 The Options menu.

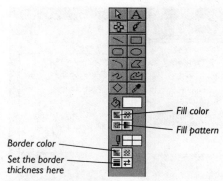

Fill color

Fill pattern

Border color

Set the border
thickness here

Figure 6.41 The Toolbox.

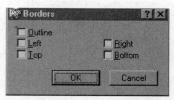

Figure 6.42 The Borders dialog box. Click the Outline, Left, Top, Right, or Bottom check boxes to obtain borders at those positions.

Figure 6.43 The Fill color palette.

Figure 6.44 The Fill pattern palette.

Borders and fills

You can dress up a spreadsheet with borders and fills. Borders are outlines around a cell, or range of cells. Fills are areas of color you can apply within a cell or range of cells.

To use borders:

1. Select the cell or range of cells where you want to have a border.

2. In the Toolbox on the left side of the spreadsheet, select the color and thickness of line you want to use (see Figure 6.41).

3. Select Borders from the Format menu. The Borders dialog box appears (see Figure 6.42).

4. Click the options for the part of the selection you want to have a border:
   –Top
   –Bottom
   –Left
   –Right
   –Outline

5. Click the OK button when you are finished.

Fills

Fills are added much the same way borders are added, but also have additional options (see Figures 6.43 and 6.44).

To add fill:

1. Select the cell, row, column or range you want to have a fill.

2. Click one of the color or pattern options from the tool palette. The color or pattern dialog box appears.

3. Click the color or the pattern you want to use. The selected area appears in that color or pattern.

Stylesheets

You can also use the predefined stylesheets to add color to your spreadsheet.

To use the stylesheets:

1. Highlight the portion of the spreadsheet you want to dress up in color.

2. Select Show Stylesheet from the Windows menu (⌘-Shift-W on the Macintosh or Control+Shift+W on Windows 95). The Stylesheet palette appears (see Figure 6.45).

3. Click the style that you want to use. The spreadsheet appears in the selected style.

4. Close the Stylesheet palette by clicking its close box.

Copying and pasting formats

Once you have the spreadsheet started you can copy much of work and use it later in the spreadsheet.

To copy formats:

1. Select the cell, row, column or range that contains the formats you want to copy.

2. Select Copy Format from the Edit menu (press Shift-⌘-C on the Macintosh or Shift+Control+C on Windows 95) (see Figure 6.46).

To paste a format:

1. To use the format, highlight the cell, row, column or range where you want to use the format.

2. Select Paste Format from the Edit menu (press Shift-⌘-V on the Macintosh or Shift+Control+V on Windows 95).

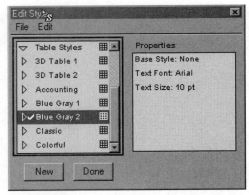

Figure 6.45 Click the stylesheet you want to use from Stylesheet palette.

Figure 6.46 Copying formats.

ADVANCED SPREADSHEETS

This chapter covers how to create charts and graphs, sort data, and how to import spreadsheets into word processing programs.

Charts and graphs

Charts and graphs are visual guides of the results obtained in any spreadsheet. There are a variety of charts and graphs available:

- Bar chart
- Area chart
- Line chart
- Scatter chart
- Pie chart
- Pictogram
- Stacked Bar
- Stacked Area
- X-Y Line chart
- X-Y Scatter
- Hi-Lo
- Stacked Pictogram

The most common are Bar charts and Pie charts.

To create a bar chart:

1. Create and save the spreadsheet, leaving it open in order to create the bar chart.

2. Highlight the chart, including all of the labels and data.

3. Choose Make Chart from the Options menu (⌘+M on the Macintosh or Control+M on Windows 95). The Chart Options dialog box appears (see Figure 7.1).

4. Click the type of chart you want to use in the Gallery pane of the Chart Options dialog box.

5. Click the OK button when you are done. The chart appears in the spreadsheet.

Positioning the chart

Charts automatically appear overlapping the highlighted information. You must move the chart to the best position so you can see both the chart and the data (see Figure 7.2).

To move a chart:

1. Click once in the middle of the chart.

2. Drag the chart where you want it on the spreadsheet.

3. Release the mouse button.

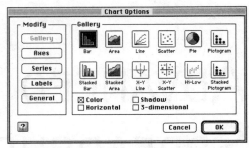

Figure 7.1 The Chart Options dialog box. Choose the type of chart you want from the Gallery.

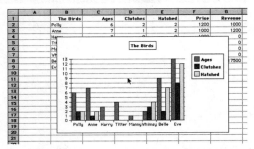

Figure 7.2 Move the new chart so it doesn't hide the data.

Chart terminology

In order to use Chart enhancements, it helps to know what different parts of a chart are called (see Figure 7.3).

- **X axis**—The horizontal line of the chart.
- **Y axis**—The vertical line of the chart.
- **Data Series**—The data you highlighted in the spreadsheet. In this example, I highlighted the names of my birds, their ages, the number of clutches each bird has laid, and the number of babies successfully hatched. This chart has three data series: age, clutches and babies.
- **Division**—Information from the spreadsheet that groups each data series. This chart's divisions are the bird's names.
- **Label**—Any text in the chart, such as titles or legends.
- **Title**—The "name" of the chart.
- **Legend**—The box that appears within the graph. Legends tell you what the bars, lines, or symbols on a chart represent.
- **Chart range**—The area of the spreadsheet that was used to create the chart.

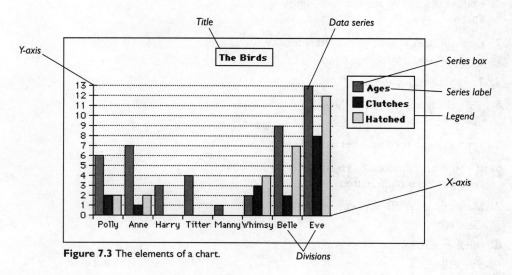

Figure 7.3 The elements of a chart.

Chart options

Chart options let you change the type of
chart, label Axes, Series, place Legends and
Titles on the chart itself.

To use chart options:

1. Double-click anywhere on the chart. The
   Chart Options dialog box appears (see
   Figure 7.4).

2. Select the Chart options you want to use
   such as Axes, Series, Label or General.

Changing the chart type

To change the chart type, just click the chart
type you want to use inside the Gallery of the
Chart Option box.

Axes options

Axes options label the vertical or horizontal
axis of the chart.

To put a label on either the X axis or the
Y axis:

1. Double-click on the chart. The Chart
   options dialog box appears (see Figure
   7.4).

2. Click the Axes button on the left side of
   the Chart options dialog box.

3. The Axis options appear.

4. Click the X axis button in the Axis
   dialog box.

5. Type a title in the Axis label box.

6. If you want to make a Y axis label,
   click the Y axis radio button.

7. Make any other changes you want to
   make.

8. Click the OK button when you are
   finished.

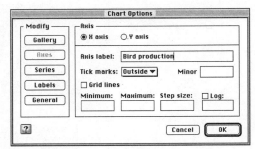

Figure 7.4 The Chart Options dialog box.

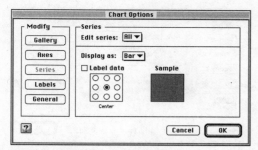

Figure 7.5 The Series Options dialog box.

Series options

Series options allow you to place the data on top of a bar by editing the series.

To edit a series:

1. Double-click on the chart. The Chart options dialog box appears.

2. Click the Series button on the left side of the Chart options dialog box.

3. The Series options appear (see Figure 7.5).

4. Select the series you want to edit from the Edit Series menu at the top of the Series pane in the Series dialog box.

5. Click the Label Data checkbox in the Series pane.

6. Select the position for the data to be placed on the bar from the position box in the Series pane of the Series dialog box.

7. Click the OK button when you are finished.

Label options

Label options allow you to set a title for the chart and position a legend.

To use Label options:

1. Double-click on the chart. The Chart options dialog box appears.

2. Click the Labels button on the left side of the Chart options dialog box.

3. The Labels options appear (see Figure 7.6).

4. Type a title for the chart in the Name box.

5. Click the Horizontal check box if you want the title to run horizontally across the top of the chart.

6. Click Shadow if you want the title to be surrounded by a box that has a drop shadow.

7. Click the position you want the title to have in the position chart.

8. If you want a legend to appear on the chart, click the legend checkbox in the bottom pane of the Labels pane.

9. Click the Horizontal checkbox if you want the legend items to appear side-by-side.

10. Click the Shadow checkbox if you want the Legend to appear surrounded by a shadowed box.

11. Click the OK button when you are finished.

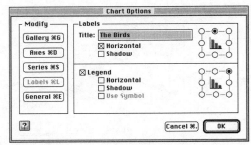

Figure 7.6 The Label Options dialog box.

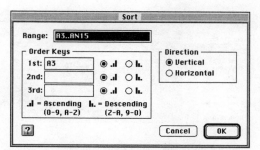

Figure 7.7 The Sort dialog box. If the data needs to be sorted in more than one way, for example, addresses that need to be sorted by state, then by zip code, enter the additional sorts in the "2nd" and "3rd" boxes.

Sorting data

You can sort spreadsheet data to arrange it in any order you wish. You may sort alphabetic or numeric information.

To sort a spreadsheet:

1. Highlight all of the data you want to sort. Include every row and all columns. But do not include column headings.

2. Select Sort from the Calculate menu (⌘-J on the Macintosh or Control+J on Windows 95). The Sort dialog box appears (see Figure 7.7).

3. In the "1st" box of the Order keys pane, type the address of a single cell in the column that you want to be sorted.

4. Click the Ascending or Descending radio button for the proper direction of the sort.

5. Click the OK button when you are finished.

SORTING DATA

Using spreadsheet data in word processing files

There are two ways to move spreadsheet data to a AppleWorks word processing document: by copying or by inserting.

To move part of a spreadsheet

1. Open the spreadsheet that contains information you want to use in a word processing document.

2. Highlight the spreadsheet information you want to use.

3. Choose Copy from the Edit menu (see Figure 7.8).

4. Close the spreadsheet.

5. Open a new word processing document or open an existing file.

6. Click where you want the word processing information to appear.

7. Choose Paste from the Edit menu. The spreadsheet appears.

8. Save the work.

To move an entire spreadsheet

1. Open the word processing document you want to contain the spreadsheet.

2. Click where you want the spreadsheet to appear.

3. Choose Insert from the File menu. The Open dialog box appears.

4. Select the spreadsheet file you want to import.

5. Click the Open button. The spreadsheet appears inside of the word processing document.

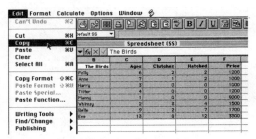

Figure 7.8 Copying part of a spreadsheet.

Name		Age	Clutches	Hatched	Price	Revenue	
African Gray	Jabri	6	2	2	1200	1000	500
B/G macaw	Bubi	7	1	2	1000	1200	600
Caique/bh	Yingwu	4	0	0	1000	0	
Greenwing Macaw	Ringo	2	0	0	1200	0	
Hyacinth Macaw	Heidi	14	0	0	6000	0	
Molacoun cockatoo	Velcro	1	0	0	1500	0	
pair fallow parrotlets	Nick	2	2	7	3500	17500	2500
pair fallow parrotlets	Grace	2			3500	0	
pair pacific parrotlets	Carl	1	3	11	100	550	50
pair pacific parrotlets	Diane	1			100	0	
pair true blue parrotlets	Einstein	2	4	17	700	8500	500
pair true blue parrotlets	Marie	2			700	0	
Severe macaw	Sweetpea	1	0	0	950	0	300

Figure 7.9 When spreadsheets are copied or imported into word processing, the column grid lines turn into tabs. The tabs separating columns of information might not be in the correct position.

African Gray	Jabri	6	2	2	1200	1000
B/G macaw	Bubi	7	1	2	1000	1200
Caique/bh	Yingwu	4	0	0	1000	0
Greenwing Macaw	Ringo	2	0	0	1200	0
Hyacinth Macaw	Heidi	14	0	0	6000	0
Molacoun cockatoo	Velcro	1	0	0	1500	0
pair fallow parrotlets	Nick	2	2	7	3500	17500
pair fallow parrotlets	Grace	2			3500	0
pair pacific parrotlets	Carl	1	3	11	100	550
pair pacific parrotlets	Diane	1			100	0
pair true blue parrotlets	Einstein	2	4	17	700	8500
pair true blue parrotlets	Marie	2			700	0
Severe macaw	Sweetpea			1	0	950	0

Figure 7.10 Highlight the data you imported. Then set tabs in the ruler to make the information appear correctly.

Dressing up imported spreadsheets

When a spreadsheet appears in a word processing document, the lines dividing the rows and columns disappear. The columns are now separated by tabs. Sometimes the tabs do not separate the columns precisely and tab settings must be adjusted.

To reformat a spreadsheet inside a word processing document:

1. Highlight the entire spreadsheet, taking care not to highlight any of the surrounding word processing text.

2. Select the proper size font for the spreadsheet so that one row will all appear on one line in the word processing document (see Figure 7.9).

3. Add new tabs if they are needed and adjust the tabs from left to right by dragging them into position on the ruler bar (see Figure 7.10).

4. Save the word processing document when you are finished.

DRESSING UP IMPORTED SPREADSHEETS

DATABASES

8

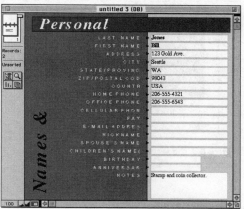

Figure 8.1 The Assistants are the easiest way to begin using the Database module of AppleWorks. These are well-designed database templates for a variety of needs.

Databases are organized collections of information, such as address lists. Some special-purpose database programs go by other names, such as "organizers." The AppleWorks database module is a general-purpose database program that lets you create organizers, appointment books, CD lists, grade books for teachers, and much more (see Figure 8.1).

Technically, a database is a file—just like a spreadsheet or a word processing document. Each file can be a different type of database.

A single database file contains multiple sets of information (such as Name, Address, City, State, Zip, and Telephone) called *records*. Each item in a record (such as the Name) is called a *field*.

Most database files contain many records (usually you have more than one person in an address list, for example). The entire collection of records is a *database*. Database programs can manipulate the data in a database (such as alphabetize all the names in an address list).

Informally, people often use the word "database" to refer to:

- The file that contains all of the fields and records.

- The program used to create database files, such as AppleWorks or FileMaker Pro.

- The actions performed by a database program.

Creating a database

AppleWorks database module allows you to set up different types of database files or use the templates that are already created for you. The Address List database is both useful and beautiful.

To use the Address List:

1. Open AppleWorks or choose New from the File menu. The Open dialog box appears.

2. Select Database from the Open File menu.

3. Click the Use Assistant or Stationery button.

4. Select Address List from the Assistant or Stationery menu. The Address List Assistant appears (see Figure 8.2).

5. Click the Next button.

6. Choose which type of address list you want (Personal, Business, or Student) to create (see Figure 8.3).

7. Click the Create button when you are finished.

Because the Address List is partially automated, it is an Assistant rather than Stationery. The Address List Assistant box walks you through setting up the database.

Figure 8.2 The Address List Assistant. Assistants are automated, with Finish, Next, and Create buttons to guide you through the steps.

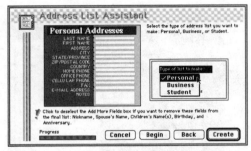

Figure 8.3 The second Assistant box lets you choose the type of address list database you wish to create.

Figure 8.4 Deleting a record.

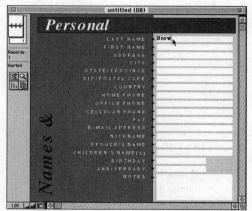

Figure 8.5 Entering the information in the "Last Name" field. Press Tab to continue to the next field.

Entering data

The Address List appears with sample data already entered. Before entering your own data you'll need to remove the sample data. The easiest way is to simply remove the records containing the sample data.

Removing records:

1. With the Address List open, select Delete Record from the Edit menu. The record disappears and the second sample record appears (see Figure 8.4).

2. Delete this second record in the same way.

Creating new records

It looks like the entire database disappeared. You see a blank piece of paper. Now we need to create a new record so you can type your own information into the Address List.

1. Select New Record from the Edit menu (⌘-R on Macintosh or Control+R on Windows 95). An empty Address List record appears.

2. Click in the first blank box on the page, the box for the Last Name information (see Figure 8.5).

3. Type the information for the first person.

4. Move to the next field by pressing the Tab key. Continue entering the information for the first person. It's okay to leave fields blank; if you do not want to enter any information for a field just press the Tab key to continue on to the next field.

5. To start a new record for a second person, Select New Record from the Edit menu.

Enter the information for the second person. And repeat steps 1 through 4 for and all other records you want to create. When you are finished with the Address List, save the file in the same way you would save a word processing file.

Moving around

Once you have created a few records, try moving between them.

To move around a database, use one of the tools or methods:

- The Rolodex
- Record number field
- The Go To Record command

Using the Rolodex

1. Select the top page of the Rolodex to move back one record (see Figure 8.6).

2. Select the bottom page of the Rolodex to move forward one record.

Using the Record number field

1. Click the Record number field at the bottom of the Rolodex (see Figure 8.7).

2. Type the record number to which you want to go.

Using the Go to Record command

1. Choose Go to Record from the Organize menu (press ⌘-G on Macintosh or Control+G on Windows 95). The Go to Record dialog box appears (see Figure 8.8).

2. Type the number of the record to which you want to move in the Go to Record dialog box.

3. Click the OK button or press Return.

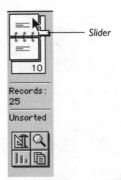

Figure 8.6 The Rolodex works just like a desktop Rolodex. Drag the slider up or down to move to the beginning or end.

Figure 8.7 Clicking on the Record Number field at the bottom of the Rolodex.

Figure 8.8 Using the Go To Record command.

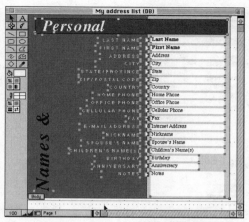

Figure 8.9 The Layout for the Address List with all objects selected.

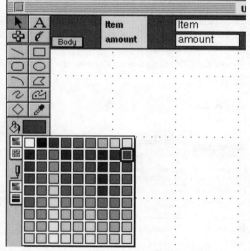

Figure 8.10 Choosing a color from the color palette.

Changing a layout

The Address List is a really good template, but it might not satisfy your needs. You can change the appearance by changing colors you do not like, making type sizes bigger or smaller, eliminating field labels or fields that you do not want to use, or adding fields to the template.

Changing area color

The template contains colors in several areas. These are just large square boxes that contain a color.

To change colors:

1. Select Layout from the Layout menu (press Shift-⌘-L on Macintosh or Shift+Control+L on Windows 95). The layout appears and you cannot see the data (see Figure 8.9).

2. Click on the layout object whose color you want to change. The handles (four small square dots) at each corner appear. This indicates that this layout object is selected.

3. Click the color palette on the left side of the layout. The color palette appears (see Figure 8.10).

4. Select the color you want the object to have. The color changes in the layout.

5. Continue with steps 1 through 4 until all colors are set the way you like.

Changing type styles

There are two kinds of type in the Address List layout:

- The text that goes in the records.

- The text in labels on the layout.

You can change both types of text using the same procedures.

To change type styles:

1. Click the field or the typed text you want to change.

2. Select Font, Size, Style, or Text Color from the Format menu. Make the changes you want to this piece of text (see Figures 8.11, 8.12, 8.13 and 8.14).

3. Click the next field or typed text you want to change and repeat step two until you are finished.

Changing field labels

You can change or erase field labels in the Layout of the Address List.

To erase a field label, click on it and press the delete or clear key.

To change text in a field label:

1. Select the "A" tool (text tool) from the tool palette on the left side of the window (see Figure 8.15).

2. Highlight the text you want to change.

3. Type the new text.

Figure 8.11 Choosing a font under the Format menu.

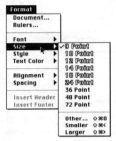

Figure 8.12 Choosing a text size under the Format menu.

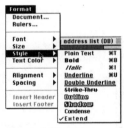

Figure 8.13 Choosing a text style under the Format menu.

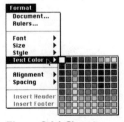

Figure 8.14 Choosing text color in the Format menu.

Figure 8.15 Selecting the text tool in the tool palette.

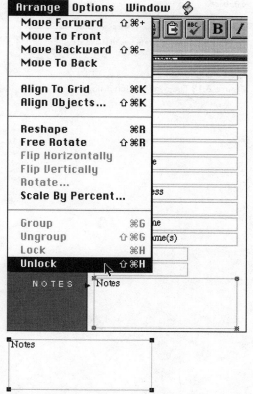

Figure 8.16 Unlocking the "Notes" field in the Address List layout (top). If the handles are gray, it's locked; if they're black, it's unlocked (bottom).

Locking and unlocking objects

Objects in a database layout may be *locked*. When you click on them, the handles are gray (instead of black). You cannot delete, move, resize, or change the colors or type styles of locked objects. You've got to *unlock* them first (see Figure 8.16). To change the appearance of a locked object, you need to unlock it.

To unlock an object:

1. Click on the object.

2. Choose Unlock under the Arrange menu (press Shift-⌘-H on Macintosh or Shift+Control+H on Windows 95).

To prevent accidentally changing an object, you can lock it. To lock an object:

1. Click on the object.

2. Choose Lock under the Arrange menu (press ⌘-H on Macintosh or Control+H on Windows 95).

Removing a field from a layout

Removing a field from a layout does not remove that field's data from the database itself. The data may still exists in the database file; but you don't have to use it in every layout for that database. For example, you probably wouldn't want to include someone's birthday on a mailing label!

To remove a field from a layout:

1. Click on the field you want to remove. If the field is locked, unlock it (press Shift-⌘-H on Macintosh or Shift+Control+H on Windows 95).

2. Press the Clear or Delete key.

Fields

Removing a field and its data from a database

Sometimes you may want to eliminate a field's data from all records in a database, not just remove the field from the database layout.

To remove fields from a database:

1. Select Define Fields from the Layout menu, or press Shift-⌘-D on the Macintosh or Shift+Control+D on Windows 95. The Define Fields dialog box appears.

2. Scroll down the Field list until you see the name of the field you want to remove.

3. Click the field name (see Figure 8.17).

4. Click the Delete button.

5. A confirmation dialog box appears (see Figure 8.18).

6. Click the OK button if you want to delete this field as well as all information that is in this field. The Define Fields dialog box reappears.

7. Click the Done button if you are finished.

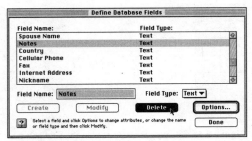

Figure 8.17 Deleting the "Notes" field from the database.

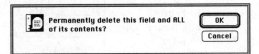

Figure 8.18 The confirmation dialog box.

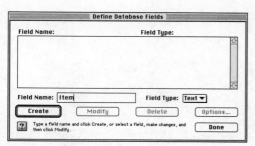

Figure 8.19 Naming a field in the Define Fields dialog box.

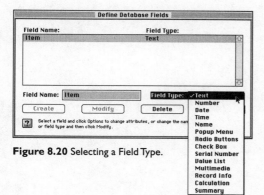

Figure 8.20 Selecting a Field Type.

Creating new fields

If you do not need all of the fields in the Address List, there might be other fields you want to add.

To add a field:

1. With the database file open, select Layout from the Layout menu. The Layout appears on the screen.

2. Select Define Fields from the Layout menu (press Shift-⌘-D on Macintosh or Shift+Control+D on Windows 95). The Define Database Fields dialog box appears.

3. Type a name for the new field in the Field Name box of the Define Database Fields dialog box (see Figure 8.19).

4. Click the Field Type pop-up menu and select the type of field you want (see Figure 8.20).

Field Types

Field type choices are:

- **Text**—All fields that contain alphabetical text or numbers that are used as text, such as zip codes.
- **Number**, **Date**, or **Time**—Uses data, time, or any numeric information. This type of field is for information that you may want to perform math on later.
- **Name**—Text field that sorts on the last word in the field.
- **Popup Menu**, or **Radio Buttons**—Fields that provide a list of choices.
- **Check Box**—Fields that produce a single-entry checkbox.
- **Serial number**—Fields contain an automatic serial number.
- **Value List**—Allows you to create a pop-up list of choices and have the database automatically enter a value if none is chosen from the list.
- **Multimedia**—A field that may contain QuickTime movies or other multimedia.
- **Record Info**—A Field that automatically enters a variety of information, such as the date a record is created.
- **Calculation**—A field into which you can enter the same types of functional formulas as in a spreadsheet.
- **Summary**—A field that allows you to summarize information by data type.

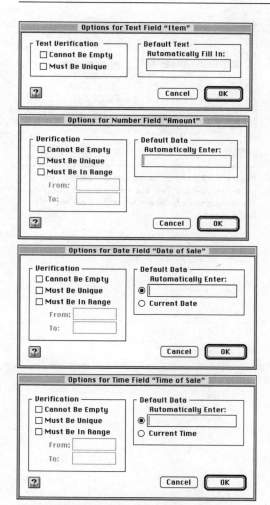

Figure 8.21 Field options for Text fields, Number fields, Date fields, and Time fields.

Text, Number, Date, Time, and Name fields

The field options for text, number, date, time, and name fields are fairly similar.

- Use the Cannot be Empty options if you wish a field to always contain information.

- Use Must be Unique if no field can contain the same information, for example, social security numbers.

- Use the Automatically Enter option to provide an default value to a field.

To use Field Options:

1. Click the Options button in the Define Database Fields dialog box. The Options dialog box opens.

2. Click one of the choices and input any necessary parameters.

3. Click the OK button when you are finished.

4. Click the Done button in the Define Database Fields dialog box if you are finished defining fields.

FIELD TYPES

Pop-up, Radio Buttons, or Value List fields

Pop-up, Radio Button, or Value List fields allow you to create menus that can be used to make data entry choices within the document. For example, you can create a menu that makes a list of student names, options for a form, or a simple yes/no field. The difference between Pop-up fields and Radio Button fields is mostly appearance.

To create Pop-up, Radio Button, or Value list fields:

1. Select Pop-up, Radio Button, or Value List from the Field Type list in the Define Database Fields dialog box. The appropriate options dialog box appears.

2. Click the Item Label field box. This is the Item that is entered into the database field as actual information when you select the item from the pop-up or value list menu or select a radio button.

3. Enter the name of the first item in the Label field (see Figure 8.22).

4. Click the Create button.

5. Click the Label field again. Enter the second item, clicking the Create button each time the label is entered into the field.

6. Click the OK button when you are finished in the dialog box.

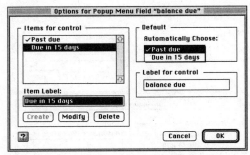

Figure 8.22 This pop up menu is completed and contains two items: Past due and Due in 15 days. Past due is automatically chosen when the New record is first created.

Checkbox or Serial Number fields

Checkbox fields allow you to create a single checkbox which can then be checked or not checked. This can be used to create fields that register information, such as whether a member's dues are paid. You can choose whether the checkbox is automatically checked upon the creation of a new field.

Serial numbers are automatically entered into a Serial number field, with the subsequent Serial number being increased by whatever increment you choose. For example, you could make the first serial number in a project be 857, and the next and subsequent serial numbers could increase by the number 6.

Record Info files

Record Info allows you to enter:

- Date Created
- Time Created
- Name of Creator
- Date Last Modified
- Time Last Modified
- Name of Modifier

You may enter only one of the choices in the Record Info field. If you need more information, such as both the Date Created and the Name of Creator, make two fields. A single field must be created for each piece of information.

Calculation and Summary fields

Calculation and Summary fields perform the same type of calculations that spreadsheets perform.

To use a calculation or summary field:

1. Select Calculation or Summary from the Field type pop-up menu in the Define Database fields pop-up box. The Enter Formula For dialog box appears (see Figure 8.23)

2. Scroll down the list of the formulas on the right side of the dialog box and select the formula you want to use.

3. Insert the names of fields in the database into the formulas. For example:

   SUM(bagels+sweet rolls)

   Use the mathematical signs that appear on the list between the list of field names and the list of formulas.

4. Click the "Format result as" pop-up menu and choose either Text, Number, Date, or Time.

5. Click the OK button when you are done.

Summary fields act like Calculation fields, but Summary fields allow you to add up all of the records for one field in the database. Calculation fields add up information for one record.

Select mathematical operators here   Select formulas from this list

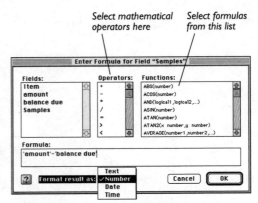

Figure 8.23 The Enter Formula For dialog box.

Changing field types

You can change field types. But be careful when doing so. Changing some types will erase all information in that field.

To change field types:

1. Select the Field Name you want to change from the Define Database Field dialog box.

2. Scroll down the Field Type pop-up menu until you see the field type you want to use.

3. Click the Modify button. A Warning dialog box tells you that any data in the field you are modifying may be permanently erased.

4. If you are certain you want to change the field type and (risk erasing all information in that field), click the OK button.

5. Click the Done button when you are finished.

Layouts

Tab order

Tab order determines which field the cursor moves to when you press the tab key. You may change the Tab order any time you want.

To change the tab order:

1. Choose Tab Order on the Layout menu. The Tab Order dialog box appears (see Figure 8.24).

2. In the Tab Order list on the right of the Tab Order dialog box, click any fields that are in the incorrect order, then click on the move button.

3. In the Tab Order list on the right of the Tab Order dialog box, select the field just below where you want your field to appear.

4. In the Field list on the left of the Tab Order dialog box, select the field you want to insert, then click the Move button. The field appears just above the field you selected in step 3.

5. Repeat steps 3 and 4 until you have moved all fields you want to move.

6. Click the OK button when you are done.

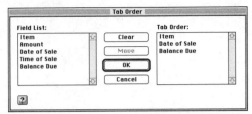

Figure 8.24 The Tab Order dialog box. The column on the right is where the cursor will appear each time the Tab key is pressed.

Figure 8.25 Selecting Layout.

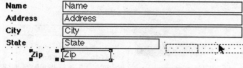

Figure 8.26 Moving a field and field label.

Positioning information

To place fields where you want them to appear in the database file, you may need to move them from their initial positions. It is easiest to move both the field and its field label at the same time. (Field labels are created automatically as you define fields.)

To move fields and labels:

1. Go to Layout view by choosing Layout under the Layout menu (see Figure 8.25).

2. Click the field you want to move.

3. Hold down the Shift key.

4. Click the field label associated with the field you want to move.

5. Let go of the Shift key.

6. Drag the field and its label to the proper position (see Figure 8.26).

7. Let go of the Mouse button when you are finished.

If you need to change color, text type or size, or fill the field with a color, do so now.

Creating sliding fields

Sliding fields do not move on the screen, but when a database is printed out, sliding fields slide up or sideways to fill the gap left by a field that contains no information.

To create a sliding object or field:

1. In the Layout view, press the Shift key and click each field in a row or a column that you want to slide if the previous or adjacent field contains no information.

2. Choose Edit Layout from the Layout menu.

3. In the Edit Layouts dialog box, click the name of the layout (see Figure 8.27).

4. Click the Modify button. The Layout Info dialog box appears (see Figure 8.28).

5. In the Layout Info dialog box, click the checkboxes labeled "Slide objects left" to close up horizontal gaps; click "Slide objects up" to close up vertical gaps.

6. Click the OK button in the Layout Information dialog box.

7. Click the OK button in the Edit Layouts dialog box.

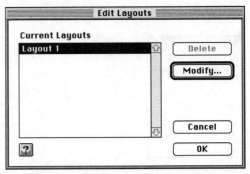

Figure 8.27 Click the layout name, then click the Modify button.

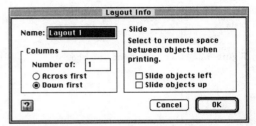

Figure 8.28 Click Slide objects left, or Slide objects up, or both.

Joe Baker	Joe Baker
Martin Van Buren	Cecilia de la Cruz
Cecilia de la Cruz	William Denver
William Denver	Joe Hughes
Joe Hughes	Robin Martinez-Vargas
John Zimmerman, III	Cynthia Moore
Robin Martinez-Vargas	Mary Smith
Cynthia Moore	Martin Van Buren
Mary Smith	John Zimmerman, III

Figure 8.29 Names in a name field. The names at left were typed using the spacebar; they sort improperly. The names at right were typed using a "hard" space in the last names; they sort well.

Figure 8.30 Duplicating a record.

Data entry tricks

Name fields that sort correctly

Name fields sort text according to the last word in the field. That works fine for names like "Mary Smith" and "Joe Hughes." But it fails with names like "Cecilia de la Cruz," "Robin Martinez-Vargas," or "Martin Van Buren." You can enter names so that they always sort correctly if you remember the following (see Figure 8.29):

1. Make sure the field type is a Name field

2. For names containing more than one word enter a *hard space* between each word instead of using the space bar (press Option-Space on Macintosh or Control+Space on Windows 95).

Duplicating information

If you are entering a series of records that contain duplicate information, duplicate a record so that the information is carried over to the next record.

To duplicate a record:

1. Click anywhere in a record that contains information you want to be the same in subsequent records.

2. Select the Duplicate Record item from the Edit menu (press ⌘-D on Macintosh or Control+D on Windows 95) (see Figure 8.30). A new duplicate record appears.

3. In the duplicated record, triple-click the field contents of any field that you want to be different and type the new information for that field.

4. Continue replacing any information you need until this record is complete.

DATA ENTRY TRICKS

139

Entering special information

Table 8.1 shows some key combinations that are useful when entering data.

Editing information in a field

Editing information within a field is done exactly the way you edit information in word processing. You can cut, copy and paste, but you can also highlight individual characters or words and type over them, apply new fonts, type sizes, or other characteristics.

Cut, Copy, and Paste

Cut, copy, and paste may be used in a AppleWorks database. Use the same procedures as in word processing:

1. Highlight the information you want to copy or cut.

2. Select Copy (⌘-C on the Macintosh or Control+C on Windows 95).

3. Click where you want the information to appear.

4. Select Paste (⌘-V on the Macintosh or Control+V on Windows 95). The text appears.

Table 8.1

Special Database Characters	
KEYS	**SPECIAL CHARACTER**
Option-space (Macintosh) or Control+Space (Windows 95)	Hard space
⌘-Hyphen (Macintosh) or Control+Hyphen (Windows 95)	Current date in a Date field
⌘-Hyphen (Macintosh) or Control+Hyphen (Windows 95)	Time field
⌘-Tab (Macintosh) or Control+Tab (Windows 95)	Tab
@ (at the beginning of an entry)	Forces the word to sort first in a Name field

Figure 8.31 Browse view.

Figure 8.32 Find view.

Figure 8.33 Layout view.

Figure 8.34 List view.

Database views

The Database can be looked at in more than one manner including:

- **Browse**—The view you use to enter information (see Figure 8.31).

- **Find**—The view you use to look for information (see Figure 8.32).

- **Layout**—The view you use to create a database (see Figure 8.33).

- **List**—The view that resembles a spreadsheet (see Figure 8.34).

These views are found under the Layout menu. Simply select the view you want to use from the Layout menu. You've already seen what the Layout view can do under "Changing a layout" earlier in this chapter. For more on the Find view, see "Using Find" later in this chapter.

Browse view

The Browse view is the view you use to enter the data.

To use the Browse view:

1. Select Browse from the Layout menu.

2. To see only one record at a time make sure Show Multiple from the Layout menu does not have a checkmark by it.

or

To see more than one record at a time, select Show Multiple on the Layout menu (see Figure 8.35).

List view

The List View looks just like a spreadsheet, and works very much like one too. You may look at records or enter in the List View.

To use the List View:

1. Choose List from the Layout menu (press Shift-⌘-L on Macintosh or Shift+Control+L on Windows 95).

2. Use the tab key to move to the right, or use Shift-tab to move to the left between fields (columns).

3. Use the up arrow to move up a row, or the down arrow to move down a row.

Moving columns in the list view

When using the List view, move the cursor close to but not on top of the line between column headings. The cursor appears as a double-sided arrow (see Figure 8.36 and 8.37). You can use this cursor to drag columns to the left or right of any column in the list.

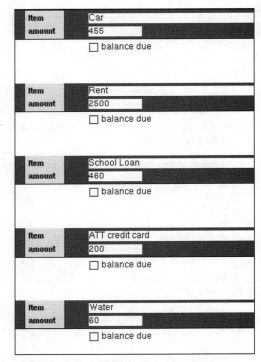

Figure 8.35 Show Multiple shows more than one record vertically on the screen in Browse view.

Item
Car
Rent
School Loan
ATT credit card
Water
Electricity

Figure 8.36 In List view, the simple double-sided cursor makes columns in the list view wider, just as it does in spreadsheets.

Item	balance due	Samples
Car		3/14/97
Rent		3/14/97
School Loan		3/14/97
ATT credit card		3/14/97
Water		3/14/97
Electricity		3/14/97
Garbage		3/14/97

Figure 8.37 In List view, the open double-sided cursor moves columns left or right.

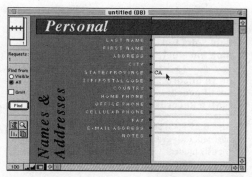

Figure 8.38 The Find view. Fill in information you are looking for in the appropriate field.

Using Find

You can use Find to locate records that:

- Match criteria
- Do not match the criteria

To find a record that matches information:

1. Select Find from the Layout menu (press Shift-⌘-F on Macintosh or Shift+Control+F on Windows 95). The Find screen appears. This screen looks like a blank record but has a different toolbox on the left side.

2. Type the information you want to find in the proper field. For example, if you wanted to find all addresses in "CA", type "CA" in the State field of the Address List database (see Figure 8.38).

3. Click the Find button on the left side of the screen, or press the Enter key. All information that matches the criteria, or the information you typed in Step 2, appears on the screen.

✔ Tips

- To tell how many records you found, look at the Rolodex on the left side of the screen. The first number under the Rolodex tells you how many records were found. The number in the parentheses tells you how many actual records exist in the total database.

- The Find feature is not case sensitive. You can type information in upper case, lower case, or mixed case.

- You do not need to type all of the information in a field to find something. The database will find partial information. For example, if you were looking for the name Jean Paul Henri-Martin, you may type any portion of that name, such as just Henri-.

Using Find and Hide Selected

Some types of queries work best if you Find the information you know you *don't* want. For example, if you wanted to look at a list of all Freshman, Sophomores, and Juniors at a high school, it is easiest to search for Seniors, then hide the information for the Seniors, leaving the information for Freshmen, Sophomores, and Juniors available for view.

If you need to look at all of the information that was *not* found, use Hide Selected from the Organize menu. This hides the information that was found and reveals the information that was not found.

To use Hide Selected:

1. Perform a Find operation.

2. Choose Select All from the Edit menu.

3. Choose Hide Selected from the Organize menu (press ⌘-Hyphen on Macintosh or Control+Hyphen on Windows 95) (see Figure 8.39).

To reveal the hidden records:

1. Choose Show All Records from the Organize menu (press Shift-⌘-A on Macintosh or Shift+Control+A on Windows 95).

Using Omit

Another way to locate the records that don't match your search criteria is to use the Omit checkbox in the Find screen's toolbox (see Figure 8.40).

Organize	Window	
Show All Records	⇧⌘A	
Hide Selected	⌘(	
Hide Unselected	⌘)	
Go To Record...	⌘G	
Sort Records...	⌘J	
Match Records...	⌘M	

Figure 8.39 Hide Selected hides records you've highlighted, and reveals the records that were previously hidden.

Figure 8.40 The Omit checkbox.

Figure 8.41 The Visible radio button.

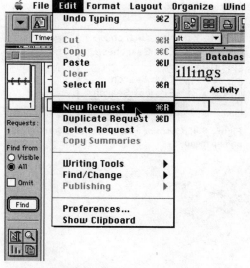

Figure 8.42 Making a New Request.

Deleting a group of Found records

Once you find the data, you may delete any records that are found:

1. Perform a Find operation.

2. Choose Select All from the Edit menu (press ⌘-A on Macintosh or Control+A on Windows 95).

3. Select Cut on the Edit menu (press ⌘-X on Macintosh or Control+X on Windows 95).

Finding within a Found set

If you find a set of information and you want to search just that set, here is how you do it:

1. Perform a Find operation. The first found set appears.

2. Perform a Second Find operation.

3. When the Find dialog box appears, click the Visible radio button on the left side of the page (see Figure 8.41).

4. Fill out the criteria in the field or fields.

5. Click the Find button when you are finished.

A two-part find

Need to do a two-part find, for example, first find everyone who lives in California, then add the people who live in Nevada, use the New Request command from the Edit menu.

1. Fill out the first set of information in the Find layout.

2. Select New Request under the Edit menu (see Figure 8.42). A blank Find layout appears.

3. Fill out the second set of information in the Find layout.

4. Press the Find button.

Saving a search

You may save the criteria in the Find form so that later when you need to search for the same item you will not have to re-create how you searched.

To save a search:

1. Perform a Find operation, but do not press the Find button.

2. Click the Spyglass on the left side of the page. The Search pop-up sub-menu appears (see Figure 8.43).

3. Select New Search. The New Search dialog box appears (see Figure 8.44).

4. Type a name for this search in the "Name for this Search" box.

5. Enter the search criteria in the search fields.

6. Click the Store button on the left side of the screen.

Using a saved search

To use a saved search:

1. Select the Search pop-up from the left side of the screen. The Search pop-up menu appears (see Figure 8.45).

2. Select the named search from the bottom of the Search pop-up menu. The search is performed for you automatically.

Figure 8.43 The Spyglass in the Search toolbox.

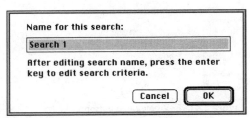

Figure 8.44 Giving a name to a search in the New Search dialog box.

Figure 8.45 Choosing a search from the Search pop-up menu.

Figure 8.46 Choosing Sort Records.

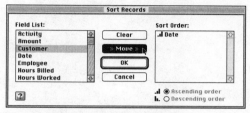

Figure 8.47 The Sort Records dialog box.

Sorting data

Sorting data arranges the information in alphabetical or numerical order.

To perform a simple sort:

1. Choose Sort Records from the Organize menu (press ⌘-J on Macintosh or Control+J on Windows 95) (see Figure 8.46).

2. In the Fields List on the left side of the Sort dialog box, click once on the field you want to sort.

3. Click the move button in the center of the Sort Records dialog box. The field appears in the list on the right side of the dialog box (see Figure 8.47).

4. Click either the Ascending or the Descending radio button.

5. Click the OK button to perform the sort.

Multiple sorts

Sometimes you need to sort more than one field at a time. For example, if you have a mailing list, you might need to sort by State first, then within the state by zip code. To perform a multiple sort:

1. Click the first field in the Sort Records dialog box and perform steps three and four above.

2. Repeat these steps until you have selected all of the fields you want to sort, in the order that they will be sorted, and complete the sort by clicking the OK button.

Changing the sort

If you want to sort by different fields, change the Sort Records dialog box.

To make changes:

1. Choose Sort Records from the Organize menu. The Sort Records dialog box appears (see Figure 8.48).

2. Click any field from the list on the right of the Sort Records dialog box.

3. Click the Clear button in the center of the Sort Records dialog box. The field now appears on the left side of the Sort Records dialog box.

4. Click any fields from the left side of the Sort Records dialog box and move them to the right side of the dialog box.

5. Click the OK button when you are finished.

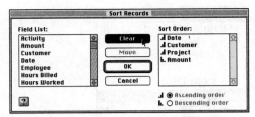

Figure 8.48 Clearing the Sort Order criteria.

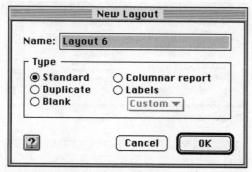

Figure 8.49 The New Layout dialog box.

Creating a new layout

Almost all of the steps you need to create a new layout may be found in the previous pages of this chapter. But here they are all in one place.

To create a new layout:

1. Select New Layout from the Layouts menu. The New Layout dialog box appears.

2. Type a name for the layout in the Name box of the New Layout dialog box (see Figure 8.49).

3. Select the type of layout you want to create from the radio buttons in the New Layout dialog box. There are five layout types:

   Standard—A blank report containing all fields

   Duplicate—A duplicate of a previous report you created. You can then edit this report and make it different for a different audience

   Blank—A blank report with no fields, art or anything

   Columnar—A report that displays fields in columns

   Labels—Creates labels using Avery sizes.

4. Click the OK button when you are done.

Once you have a new layout, you may:

- Add new fields and labels.

- Change fonts, type size, or text color.

- Change the tab order of the fields.

- Add graphics, background color, or other enhancements.

- Create summary fields to add all of the records together.

Parts of a new layout

Layout parts control how information is calculated and how it appears on the screen. There are five major parts:

- **Header**—includes any information you want printed at the top of every page (page number, date, time, text)
- **Leading grand summary**—creates report sections (such as first quarter sales, second quarter sales from the "quarters" field)
- **Subsummary when sorted by**—which adds up subtotals (for example, sort by a field called "bracelets" and use the field called "bracelets" in a Subsummary field to create a subtotal)
- **Trailing grand summary**—adds up calculated fields for individual items, such as when you want to find out how many sales each individual employee made (when employee is a field and individual names are entered in the employee field)
- **Footer**—includes any information you want printed at the bottom of every page (page number, date, time, text)

Creating parts

To create a part:

1. In the Layout view, choose Insert Part from the Layout menu. The Insert Part dialog appears (see Figure 8.50).

2. In the Insert Part dialog box, select the radio button that describes the type of part you want to use.

3. Click the OK button in the Insert Part dialog box when you are finished.

4. To resize a part, select the solid line that defines the bottom of the part and that has the part label on the left side of the layout (see Figure 8.51).

5. Drag up or down until the part is the size you want it to be.

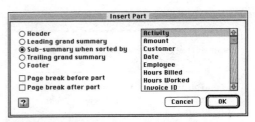

Figure 8.50 The Insert Part dialog box.

Figure 8.51 Moving a part.

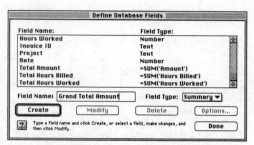

Figure 8.52 Creating a Summary field.

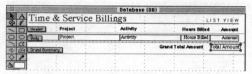

Figure 8.53 Creating a Grand Summary part.

Figure 8.54 The Print dialog box.

Creating a summary report

Summary reports add up data. Summary reports use number, calculation, and summary fields, and place summary information in Grand summary sections. Here is a quick guide to a simple summary report.

To create a summary report:

1. Create your new report with fields for items that need to be input.

2. Create a calculation field.

3. Create an summary field that adds up all of the calculation fields (see Figure 8.52).

4. Create a Grand Summary part at the bottom of the report and place the Summary field in that part (see Figure 8.53).

Printing a database

You can print the entire database, a few records, or just one record.

To print:

1. Choose Print from the File menu. The Print dialog box appears (see Figure 8.54).

2. Click either the "Current Record" or "Visible Records' radio button in the Print dialog box.

   Choosing "Current Record" prints the record that is selected. Choosing "Visible Records" prints all records that are visible.

3. Click the Print button.

Importing and exporting data

Importing and exporting information between databases is usually fairly easy.

To export data from AppleWorks database, use Save As from the File menu and save the work as a Comma Values Macintosh or Comma Values DOS file. The file should then easily transfer to any database program.

If you export data to a word processing program, you'll find that columns seldom line up properly in the word processing document. You need to highlight the information when it is imported into the Word Processing module. Once you have highlighted information, you need to insert tabs to make the information line up properly (see Figures 8.55 and 8.56).

To import a file from another program, check the exporting procedures in that program's manual. If there are no procedures, try and find "export" on a File menu and translate the file as a Comma Values or Comma Separated Values file.

To import a file that does not have a template in AppleWorks, first create a new database file that contains fields and field names. Create as many fields as you think you might need. You may always edit the fields and field names later.

To bring a Comma Values (or CSV) file into AppleWorks database:

1. Choose Insert from the File menu. The Open files dialog box appears.

2. Select the file you want to use. The file opens in AppleWorks Database.

Name		Age	Clutches	Hatched	Price	Revenue	
African Gray	Jabri	6	2	2	1200	1000	500
B/G macaw	Bubi	7	1	2	1000	1200	600
Caique/bh	Yingwu	4	0	0	1000	0	
Greenwing Macaw	Ringo		2	0	0	1200	0
Hyacinth Macaw	Heidi		14	0	0	6000	0
Molaccun cockatoo	Veloro		1	0	0	1500	0
pair fallow parrotlets	Nick		2	2	7	3500	17500	2500
pair fallow parrotlets	Grace		2			3500	0
pair pacific parrotlets	Carl		1	3	11	100	550	50
pair pacific parrotlets	Diane		1			100	0
pair true blue parrotlets	Einstein		2	4	17	700	8500	500
pair true blue parrotlets	Marie		2			700	0
Severe macaw	Sweetpea		1	0	0	950	0	300

Figure 8.55 When database information is imported into word processing the columns no longer line up.

African Gray	Jabri	6	2	2	1200	1000
B/G macaw	Bubi	7	1	2	1000	1200
Caique/bh	Yingwu	4	0	0	1000	0
Greenwing Macaw	Ringo	2	0	0	1200	0
Hyacinth Macaw	Heidi	14	0	0	6000	0
Molaccun cockatoo	Veloro	1	0	0	1500	0
pair fallow parrotlets	Nick	2	2	7	3500	17500
pair fallow parrotlets	Grace	2			3500	0
pair pacific parrotlets	Carl	1	3	11	100	550
pair pacific parrotlets	Diane	1			100	0
pair true blue parrotlets	Einstein	2	4	17	700	8500
pair true blue parrotlets	Marie	2			700	0
Severe macaw	Sweetpea	1	0		0	950

Figure 8.56 Highlight the data, then insert tabs to make columns line up properly.

9

DRAWING

AppleWorks has two art modules, Drawing and Painting. While you can create pictures using either one, they construct the images differently and each has its own style, just as painting and drawing on paper are somewhat different.

In AppleWorks, drawing creates object-oriented graphics, while Painting creates bit-mapped graphics. Pictures drawn in the Draw module are composed of separate objects, while pictures created in the Paint module are just one object. You'll want to experiment with both modules. The actual procedures to create graphics in either Drawing or Painting are almost identical, however.

Drawing tools

Drawing and Painting tools are almost identical, so the tools common to both modules are covered in this chapter. (For tools used only in Painting, see Chapter 10). Each tool in the toolbox has a specific function (see Figure 9.1).

Pointer tool

The pointer tool is used to select objects. Objects may then be moved or deleted.

To select an object:

1. Select the pointer tool from the toolbox.

2. Click in the middle of an object. Dots appear on its perimeter. These dots indicate the object is selected (see Figure 9.2)

Text tool

The text tool is used to add text to drawing (see Figure 9.3).

To insert text into a picture:

1. Select the text tool from the toolbox.

2. Click on the picture where you want the text to appear.

3. Type the text.

4. Select the pointer or another tool to get out of Text mode.

If you insert text, you'll want to format the text to suit your design.

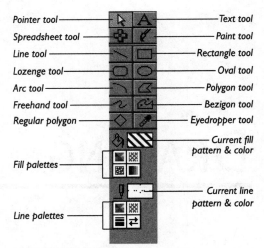

Pointer tool — Text tool
Spreadsheet tool — Paint tool
Line tool — Rectangle tool
Lozenge tool — Oval tool
Arc tool — Polygon tool
Freehand tool — Bezigon tool
Regular polygon — Eyedropper tool
Current fill pattern & color
Fill palettes
Current line pattern & color
Line palettes

Figure 9.1 The Drawing toolbox.

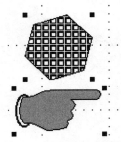

Figure 9.2 Dots appear on the edges of all selected objects, whether the object is a piece of clipart, rectangle, oval, or polygon.

Figure 9.3 The text tool looks like a capital "A." The text tool creates text that does not automatically word wrap in a drawing.

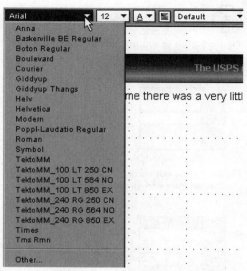

Figure 9.4 The Font menu is the same in all AppleWorks modules.

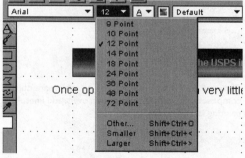

Figure 9.5 The Size menu. Choose "other" at the bottom of the menu if you need a size that isn't listed.

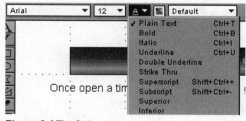

Figure 9.6 The Style menu.

To change text appearance in a drawing:

1. Select the text tool from the toolbox.

2. Triple-click inside of the text to select the entire line, or double-click inside a word to select a word.

3. Choose the font you want to use from the Font menu, or by clicking the Font popup menu on the main menu bar (see Figure 9.4).

4. Choose the size of font you want to use from the Size menu, or by clicking the Size popup menu on the main menu bar (see Figure 9.5).

5. Choose Bold, Italic, Underline, or Outline styles by clicking the Enhancement popup menu on the main menu bar (see Figure 9.6).

6. Choose the color for the text from the Color palette on the Button Bar. To choose a background color for text, click on the pointer tool and select a color from the Color palette in the toolbox (see Figure 9.7).

✔ Tip

■ You can create a mini word processing document inside a drawing by clicking and dragging a rectangle with the Text tool.

Figure 9.7 To change the text color select the color palette on the Button Bar. To change the background color, use the Pointer tool and select the color palette in the toolbox.

DRAWING TOOLS

Insert Spreadsheet tool

You can insert spreadsheets into a drawing and enter information and formulas as if you were in the Spreadsheet module.

1. Select the Insert Spreadsheet tool from the toolbox. The pointer changes to a thick spreadsheet cross pointer (see Figure 9.8).

2. Drag the pointer from the upper right to the lower left to create a spreadsheet rectangle. A blank spreadsheet appears in the rectangle you've drawn (see Figure 9.9).

3. Click on the first cell of the spreadsheet where you want to enter information. The main toolbar changes to the spreadsheet toolbar.

4. Enter the spreadsheet information, data, formulas, and formatting.

5. Click outside the spreadsheet when you are done. The drawing toolbar reappears.

To move a spreadsheet within Drawing:

1. Select the pointer tool from the toolbox.

2. Click the top gray bar in the spreadsheet. The selection dots appear (see Figure 9.10).

3. Tap the Clear or Delete button or choose Cut from the Edit menu. Macintosh users may press ⌘-X, Windows 95 users may press Control+X.

Paint tool

The paint tool in the toolbox allows you to place paint documents into a draw document.

To use the paint tool:

1. Click the paint tool in the toolbox (see Figure 9.11).

2. Click and drag in the document to place a paint style rectangle.

For information on how to paint, see Chapter 10, "Painting."

Figure 9.8 The spreadsheet pointer looks exactly the spreadsheet tool in the toolbox.

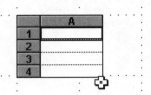

Figure 9.9 You may make the spreadsheet as large as you like, but leave enough room for the drawing, too.

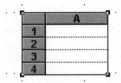

Figure 9.10 When you select the spreadsheet with the pointer tool, it becomes an object just like a picture or rectangle.

Figure 9.11 When you paint you do not create objects composed of pieces like rectangles, ovals, and lines. A painting is a single object.

DRAWING TOOLS

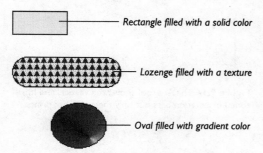

Rectangle filled with a solid color

Lozenge filled with a texture

Oval filled with gradient color

Figure 9.12 The Lozenge is just a rectangle with rounded corners.

Size
⊢	1.25 in
T	9.25 in
→|	3.36 in
↓	9.83 in
↔	2.11 in
⇕	0.58 in
↻	0°

Figure 9.13 The Object Size palette.

Object tools

Object tools include tools to make lines, rectangles, ovals, or freeform figures.

Line tool

To use the line tool:

1. Click the line tool in the toolbox. The cross-hair pointer (+) appears.

2. Click where you want the line to begin.

3. Hold the mouse button down.

4. Drag until the line is as long as you want.

✔ Tip

■ Hold the Shift key down while you are dragging to keep the line horizontal, vertical, or diagonal.

Rectangle, Lozenge and Circle tools

The rectangle, lozenge, and circle tools create enclosed objects that may be filled with color, patterns, and textures. These objects may be stacked on top of one another in such a way that they create the illusion of a new object.

To create a rectangle, lozenge, or circle (see Figure 9.12):

1. Select the rectangle, lozenge, or circle tool from the toolbox. The cross-hair pointer (+) appears.

2. Click in the document where you want to draw the rectangle, lozenge, or circle.

3. Drag until the object is the appropriate size.

✔ Tip

■ To find out the exact size of the object, choose the object and then select Object Size from the Options menu. The size, location, and rotation of the object appear in the Object Size palette. To change the object size, location, or rotation, select any of the current measurements and type a new measurement (see Figure 9.13).

OBJECT TOOLS

157

Arc tool

The Arc tool creates curved lines based on geometrical principles (see Figure 9.14).

To create an arc:

1. Select the Arc tool from the toolbox.

2. Click where you want the line to begin.

3. Drag until the line is about the right width. Keep the mouse button down. The indicator lines appear.

4. Adjust the line up or down until the indicator lines and the arc fit what is needed for the document.

5. Let go of the mouse button. The indicator lines disappear.

Sometimes arcs need to be made smaller or larger.

To change the size or shape of an arc:

1. Select the Arc tool from the toolbox. Dots appear at the four corners of the line and where the indicator lines normally appear. The indicator lines appear in light gray (see Figure 9.15).

2. Select one of the corner dots.

3. Drag the dot up, down, left, or right until the curved line is the appropriate size and shape.

Figure 9.14 The Arc tool shows the vertical and horizontal orientation bars but only the actual arc prints.

Figure 9.15 Once you click on the arc with the pointer tool, you see the corner dots.

Figure 9.16 The Polygon Tool

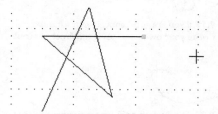

Figure 9.17 Lines are continuous, but are formed in sections. You can see the beginning of a section by looking for a node, or dot on a line.

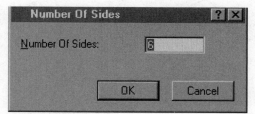

Figure 9.18 Type the number of sides you want the polygon to have in the Polygon Side dialog box.

Polygon tool

A polygon is a many-sided, irregularly shaped, object. Like the other drawing objects, polygons may be filled with color, patterns, or textures. Making polygons is a bit like the child's connect-the-dots game, where you are making the dots and the Polygon tool connects them for you.

To create a polygon:

1. Select the Polygon tool from the toolbox (see Figure 9.16).

2. Click where you want the outline of the object to begin.

3. Click where you want that portion of the line to end.

4. Click where you want the next section of the line to end (see Figure 9.17).

5. Continue clicking until the entire shape is formed. To enclose the polygon, make sure the final line joins the beginning.

Regular Polygon tool

The regular polygon tool draws many-sided objects. Each side of the object is equal, and all sides are straight. To draw a regular polygon:

1. Select Polygon Sides from the Edit menu. The Polygon Side dialog box appears (see Figure 9.18).

2. Type the number of sides you want in the number box (3 for a triangle, etc.).

3. Click the OK button.

4. Click the Polygon tool in the toolbox. The cross-hair pointer (+) appears.

5. Drag in the document until the regular polygon is the intended size.

Moving and deleting regular polygons is accomplished in the same way as moving rectangles, lozenges, or ovals.

OBJECT TOOLS

Freehand tool

The Freehand tool lets you draw lines that are not straight. That is, the lines may be drawn as freely as you would draw with pencil on paper (see Figure 9.19).

To draw with the Freehand tool:

1. Click the Freehand tool. The cross-hair pointer (+) appears.

2. Move the pointer to form the shape you want.

✔ Tip

■ You can even sign your name with the Freehand tool if you can control the mouse that well.

Bezigon tool

The Bezigon tool draws gently curved lines that extend between points where you click.

To use the Bezigon tool:

1. Click the Bezigon tool. The cross-hair cursor (+) appears.

2. Click where you want the shape to begin.

3. Click where you want the first segment to end (see Figure 9.20).

4. Click at every point where you want the curve to assume another direction. A "node" is formed at this point. The nodes can be used later to edit a bezier line (see Figure 9.21).

5. Double-click when you are finished.

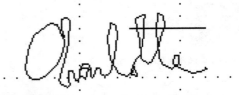

Figure 9.19 If you are good enough with a mouse, you can even write your own name using the Freehand tool.

Figure 9.20 The Bezigon tool starts with handles that are used to manipulate lines into curves.

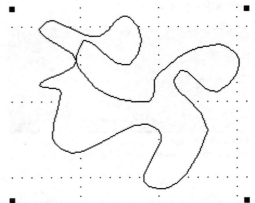

Figure 9.21 Nodes can be created in a bezigon line by double-clicking any point on the line. A new node is formed.

Figure 9.22 Bezigons do not have to be closed objects. Open or closed, the four dots describe the four corners of an object.

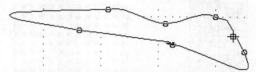

Figure 9.23 The cross-hair cursor indicates you may reshape an item by dragging on one of the nodes.

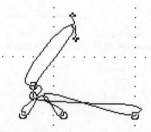

Figure 9.24 Pull up or down by clicking on the node the dragging up or down to stretch the line.

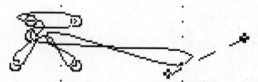

Figure 9.25 Tangents are control handles that allow you to apply a twist to a line. To use a tangent, click on one of the ends of the straight line, then move the handle in the direction you want to apply a twist.

Editing Bezigons

Bezigons are edited by manipulating the nodes that are formed every time you click the mouse.

To edit a bezigon:

1. Select the Pointer tool from the toolbox.

2. Click the bezigon. Four dots appear on the four corners of the object (see Figure 9.22).

3. Select Reshape from the Arrange menu (press ⌘-R on the Macintosh or Control+R on Windows 95). The nodes in the line appear and the pointer changes to the cross-hair pointer with a square box in the center (see Figure 9.23).

4. Click a node and pull up, down, left, or right to stretch the curve in the appropriate direction (see Figure 9.24).

5. Click the left or right handle of the tangent that extends from the node.

6. Twist the tangent up, down, left, or right to apply a twist to the line (see Figure 9.25).

7. Select another drawing tool or double-click outside of the bezigon to finish editing.

Eyedropper tool

The Eyedropper tool (see Figure 9.26) is more of a shortcut than a tool that performs a special function. If you have ever used a photo-manipulation program, you are probably familiar with the concept of an Eyedropper.

Eyedroppers pick up color, pattern, or texture attributes from objects that are already colored or filled with colors, patterns, or textures. Once the attribute is picked up, the next object you draw is filled with it.

To use the Eyedropper tool:

1. Click the Eyedropper tool in the toolbox. The eyedropper pointer appears.

2. Click the color, pattern, or texture you want to borrow. The Paint Bucket is filled with that attribute (see Figure 9.27).

3. Draw any new object and it will be filled with the chosen attribute.

Figure 9.26 The Eyedropper tool picks up any color, texture or pattern that is used in an object.

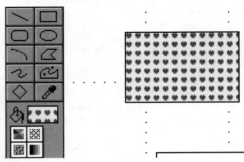

Figure 9.27 The paint bucket indicator tells you what pattern, texture, or color will fill the next object that is drawn.

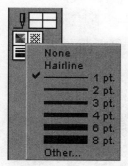

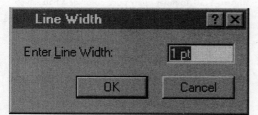

Figure 9.28 Use hairline for professional looking lines. This is the preferred size of fine book publishers.

Figure 9.29 You do not need to type "pt" after the measurement. The measurements in this box are in points, a typographical measurement. There are 72 points to an inch, 36 points to a half inch, and 18 points to one-quarter of an inch.

Line attributes

Lines can have varying thicknesses, colors, and patterns. And you can add arrow heads to lines.

Line thickness

Line thickness goes from hairline (or .3 of a point) to 8 points on the line thickness popup menu. But you may also specify any line thickness you like by choosing "Other" on the line thickness popup menu (see Figure 9.28).

To change line thickness:

1. Select the line by using the pointer tool. Selection dots appear at either end of the line.

2. Click the Line Thickness popup menu in the toolbox panel. The popup menu appears.

3. Choose the selection you want to use for the line.

   or

   Choose "Other" and enter a thickness in the Line Width dialog box (see Figure 9.29).

Line color and pattern

You may add color and pattern to lines.

To add a color to a line:

1. Select the line.

2. Click the color palette in the toolbox panel. The color palette popup appears.

3. Select the color you want the line to be. Any arrows that the line has also change to this color.

To add a pattern to a line:

1. Select the line.

2. Click the pattern palette in the toolbox panel. The pattern palette popup appears (see Figure 9.30).

3. Select the pattern you want the line to have. Any arrows that the line has also change to this pattern. If you previously or subsequently change the line to a color, the pattern also appears in the color.

Adding arrows

You can add pre-made arrows to the ends of lines created with the Line tool.

To add arrows:

1. Draw a line with the line tool.

2. Click the Arrow popup menu in the toolbox panel. The Arrow popup menu appears (see Figure 9.31).

3. Select the type of arrow you want to apply to this line. Your choices are: Plain Line, Arrow At Start, Arrow At End, and Arrow At Both Ends.

✔ Tip

■ If you don't know which is the Start or End of the line and the arrow appears at the wrong end of the line, reselect the line and make another choice.

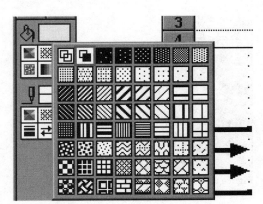

Figure 9.30 You may apply pure color or a pattern to arrows, but not gradients or textures.

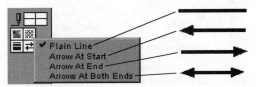

Figure 9.31 Arrow At Start means the arrowhead appears where you first clicked to draw the line. Arrow At End means the arrowhead appears where you stopped.

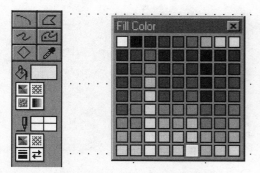

Figure 9.32 Click on the grey outline of the color, texture, pattern, or gradient palette, then drag the palette into the middle of the document.

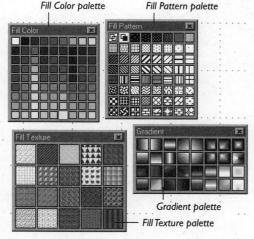

Fill Color palette   *Fill Pattern palette*

Gradient palette

Fill Texture palette

Figure 9.33 Object fill palettes.

Object attributes

Color, gradient, pattern, and texture

To fill an object with a color, gradient, pattern, or texture:

1. Select the pointer tool from the toolbox.

2. Select the object.

3. Click the color, gradient, pattern, or texture popup menu in the toolbar pane (see Figure 9.32).

4. Click the color, gradient, pattern or texture that you want to use from the appropriate palette (see Figure 9.33).

Changing the outline

Outlines are the lines that surround an object. The default outline is 1 point and appears in black.

To change the outline of an object:

1. Select the pointer tool from the toolbox.

2. Select the object.

3. Click the Line Thickness popup menu in the toolbox panel. The popup menu appears.

4. Click the selection you want to use for the line.

Outline color

Outlines may have color and pattern as easily as objects or free standing lines.

To add color to an outline:

1. Select the object.

2. Select the color palette in the toolbox panel. The color palette appears.

3. Select the color you want to use for the outline.

OBJECT ATTRIBUTES

Making changes

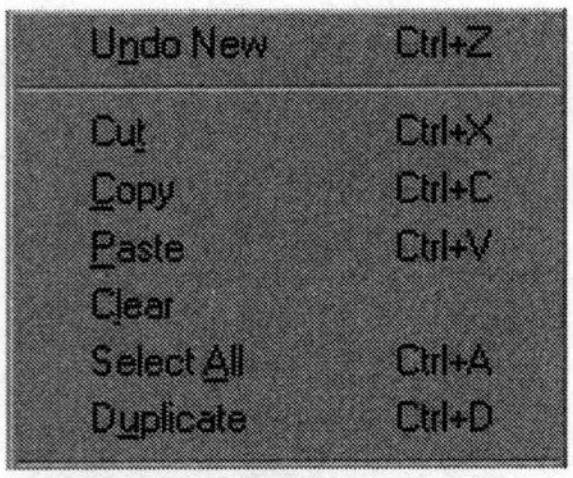

Most changes are made on the Arrange or
Options menus. Changes you can make
include:

- Deleting an object
- Moving an object
- Stacking objects up in a different order
- Aligning objects
- Reshaping an object (not available with
  all objects)
- Rotating an object
- Flipping an object (horizontally or
  vertically)
- Scaling an object
- Locking an object (so no changes may
  be made)
- Resizing an object
- Changing the text wrap

Figure 9.34 The Edit menu.

Deleting and moving objects

To delete an object:

1. Select the object.

2. Press the Clear or Delete key, or select Cut
   from the Edit menu. You may also press
   ⌘-X on the Macintosh or Control+X on
   Windows 95 (see Figure 9.34). The object
   is deleted.

✔ Tip

- When an object is deleted using cut, it is
  placed on the Clipboard and is available to
  be pasted elsewhere in the document. You
  may even paste the cut object into a word
  processing, spreadsheet, or database file.

To move an object:

1. Select the object.

2. Place the pointer in the middle of the
   object and hold down the mouse button.

3. Drag the object into the appropriate
   position.

MAKING CHANGES

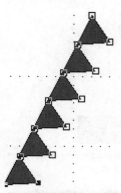

Figure 9.35 Duplicating an object.

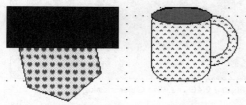

Figure 9.36 The box is stacked on top of a many-sided regular polygon. The coffee cup is made up of four separate objects: an oval for the top, a lozenge for the body, and two circles, one filled with white, for the handles.

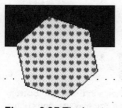

Figure 9.37 The box is moved behind the regular polygon.

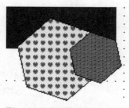

Figure 9.38 The box is behind two other objects, so it is moved to the back, not just backwards.

Duplicating objects

To duplicate an object:

1. Select the object to be duplicated.

2. Choose Duplicate from the Edit menu (see Figure 9.35).

3. Move the new, duplicated object where you want it to appear.

Stacking objects

Drawing objects may be stacked on top of each other (see Figure 9.36).

To stack objects, drag one object on top of a second object. The item might still not appear correctly. Objects must be stacked in the proper order for the new multi-part object to look right.

To rearrange stacked objects by moving one object behind other objects:

1. Click the object that needs to be moved.

2. Select Move Backward from the Arrange menu (press Shift-⌘-Hypen on the Macintosh or Shift+Control+Hyphen on Windows 95). The selected object is moved back a layer (see Figure 9.37).

To rearrange stacked objects by moving an object behind all other objects:

1. Click the object that needs to be moved.

2. Select Move to Back from the Arrange menu. The selected object moves underneath all other objects (see Figure 9.38).

DUPLICATING OBJECTS

Aligning objects

It is difficult to make sure all objects are lined up precisely when doing a drawing (or a painting). There are two ways to line them up:

Aligning objects to the grid:

1. Select Show Graphics Grid from the Options menu. The grid appears as a dotted lines. The grid does not print; it is simply a guide to help you align objects (see Figure 9.39).

2. Select an object.

3. Select Align to Grid under the Arrange menu.

Aligning objects with each other:

1. Select all of the objects you want to align.

2. Select Align Objects from the Arrange menu (press Shift-⌘-K on the Macintosh or Shift+Control+K on Windows 95). The Align dialog box appears (see Figure 9.40).

3. Click the appropriate choices in the Top to Bottom and Left to Right pane of the Align dialog box (see Figure 9.41).

4. Click the Apply button to preview how they'll look when aligned.

5. Click the OK button when you are done.

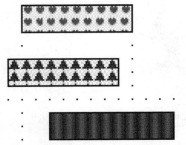

Figure 9.39 The grid appears as light grey dotted lines and is used to help you line up objects.

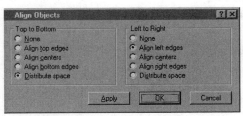

Figure 9.40 The Align Objects dialog box.

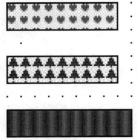

Figure 9.41 Use only one choice in the Top to Bottom pane, or the Left to Right pane. You may use one choice from each pane, such Align bottom edges from the Top to Bottom pane and Align top edges from the Left to Right pane.

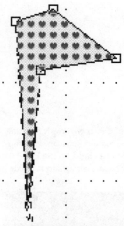

Figure 9.42 You may freely edit all nodes, and form new nodes by double-clicking any point in the line.

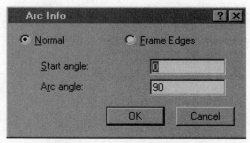

Figure 9.43 The Frame edges radio button makes the straight edges show up as regular lines.

Reshaping an object

Reshaping is only one way to change an object. You may also use:

- Arc info on the Edit menu for arcs.

- Smooth or Unsmooth from the Edit menu for all shapes.

- Corner Info from the Edit menu to make rounded corners with rectangles or square corners with lozenges.

To reshape an arc, polygon, bezigon, or free-hand shape:

1. Select the pointer tool in the toolbox.

2. Select the object you want to reshape.

3. Select Reshape from the Arrange menu (press ⌘-R on the Macintosh or Control+R on Windows 95).

4. Click on any node and drag the node up, down, left, or right to reshape the node.

5. Repeat step four until you are finished (see Figure 9.42).

Arc Info

To use Arc Info:

1. Select any arc in the drawing.

2. Select Arc Info from the Edit menu. The Arc Info dialog box appears (see Figure 9.43).

3. Select the Frame edges radio button to make the angles that support the arc appear as solid lines.

4. Type the appropriate numbers in the Start angle and Arc angle boxes.

5. Click OK when you are finished.

Smooth

Smooth makes irregular edges smooth:

To use smooth:

1. Select the object you want to smooth.

2. Select Smooth from the Edit menu. The object is smoothed (see Figure 9.44).

Be very careful with smooth because it can make radical changes to any drawing.

Changing corners

The Rectangle tool draws boxes with 90 degree corners and the Lozenge tools draws boxes with rounded corners. You may round the corners of any rectangle or change the rounding on lozenges.

To change corners:

1. Select the object you want to have round corners.

2. Select Corner Info from the Edit menu. The Corner Info dialog box appears (see Figure 9.45).

3. Type the radius, or curve, you want the object to have in the Radius box.

   or

   Click Round Ends make the narrow ends of the object into semicircles.

4. Click the OK button when you are done. The rectangle now has rounded corners

✔ Tip

- A good number to type in the radius box is 15. This gives pleasantly but strongly rounded.

- If you change the Corner Info number to 0, a lozenge becomes a rectangle.

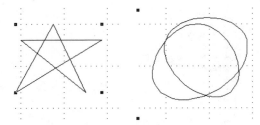

Figure 9.44 The star is turned into two ovals by using smooth. Smooth can have extreme results on drawings if you are not careful. You can use Undo on the Edit menu to reverse a Smooth action that you do not like.

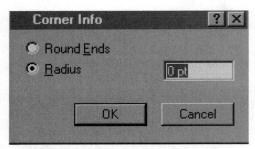

Figure 9.45 The Corner Info dialog box.

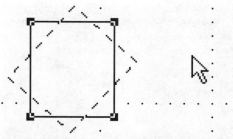

Figure 9.46 To use Free Rotate, click on one of the corner dots and drag the object into the proper rotation.

Figure 9.47 The Rotate dialog box lets you rotate an object by typing in the degrees of rotation, such as 90 for a quarter turn. You do not need to type in any degree sign.

Original   *Flip Horizontal*   *Flip Vertical*

Figure 9.48 The original frog faces left.

Rotating an object

You can rotate an object to any angle.

To rotate an object:

1. Select the object.

2. Select Free Rotate from the Arrange menu (press Shift-⌘-R on the Macintosh or Shift+Control+R on Windows 95).

3. Select one of the corner handles and drag the object into the rotation you want (see Figure 9.46).

Rotating by measurement

You can also specify a degree of rotation.

To rotate by measurement:

1. Select the object you want to rotate.

2. Select Rotate from the Arrange menu. The Rotate dialog box appears (see Figure 9.47).

3. Type the degree of rotation you want the object to have in the Rotate dialog box.

4. Click the OK button when you are finished.

Flipping an object

Objects may be oriented vertically or horizontally by using the flip commands, Flip Horizontally and Flip Vertically.

To flip an object:

1. Select the object you want to flip (see Figure 9.48).

2. Select Flip Horizontally to flip the object horizontally.

   or

   Select Flip Vertically to turn the object upside down.

Scaling an object

Scaling an object is how you change the size of the object.

To scale an object:

1. Select the object you want to scale.

2. Select Scale by Percent from the Arrange menu. The Scale by Percent dialog box appears (see Figure 9.49).

3. Type the percentage you want the height to increase in the height box.

4. Type the percentage you want the width to increase in the width box.

5. Click the OK button when you are finished.

Locking an object

Locking prevents changes from being made to an object.

To lock an object:

1. Select the object you want to lock.

2. Select Lock from the Arrange menu. The object is locked and the corner dots appear light grey.

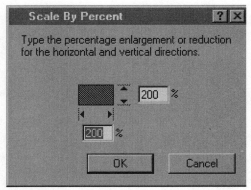

Figure 9.49 The right box in the Scale by Percent dialog box changes the height of an object. The bottom box in the Scale by Percent dialog box changes the width of an object.

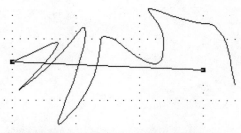

Figure 9.50 Reshaping and connecting is kind of tricky. The important thing is to remember to select Reshape from the Arrange menu just after you select the object. Once the commands are completed, the two objects become one.

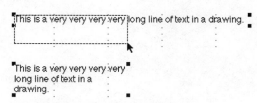

Figure 9.51 Changing the text wrap.

Connecting objects

When you make an object, you may need to use the bezigon, polygon, or freehand tools, but each object is a separate object. You may connect any of these individual objects into one object.

To connect objects:

1. Select the first object.

2. Choose Reshape from the Arrange menu. The corner dots turn into anchor points and the reshape pointer appears (see Figure 9.50).

3. Choose Cut or Copy from the Edit menu.

4. Select the point on the second object where you want the first object to be connected.

5. Choose Paste from the Edit menu.

6. Choose Reshape from the Arrange menu.

Changing the text wrap

To change the text wrap:

1. With the pointer tool, select the text. Handles appear.

2. Grab a handle and move it where you'd like. The text rewraps automatically (see Figure 9.51).

PAINTING

Painting works very much like Drawing, but the pictures created are not made up of individual objects. Instead, each picture is made up of pixels, or small dots, that form the shapes. In Drawing you can move an oval or rectangle, for example, but because the shapes in Painting are made up of pixels, you cannot move them. You may only pick up one pixel at a time.

Painting tools

Painting uses almost the same tools as Drawing so this chapter only covers tools unique to Painting (see Figure 10.1). Refer to Chapter 9 for descriptions of the other tools.

Selection Rectangle tool

The Selection Rectangle tool is used to select part or all of an image.

To use the Selection Rectangle tool:

1. Click the Selection Rectangle tool in the Toolbox.

2. Drag the Selection Rectangle tool until the dotted outline surrounds the object (see Figure 10.2).

or

Select the Outline of an object by holding the ⌘ key down on the Macintosh while dragging the Selection Rectangle tool, or holding the Control key down in Windows 95.

To select everything in the document, double-click the Selection Rectangle.

Lasso tool

The Lasso tool is a freehand-style selection tool.

To use the Lasso tool:

1. Click the Lasso tool in the Toolbox.

2. Drag the Lasso tool around the object you want to select. It closes the line automatically (see Figure 10.3).

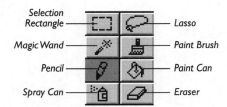

Figure 10.1 The Painting tools.

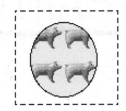

Figure 10.2 Using the Selection Rectangle.

Figure 10.3 Using the Lasso tool.

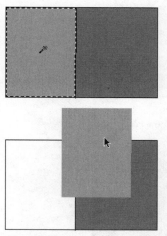

Figure 10.4 Selecting a color with the Magic Wand (top) and moving the selection (bottom).

Figure 10.5 Using the Brush tool.

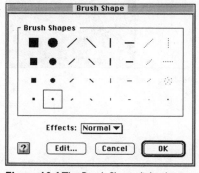

Figure 10.6 The Brush Shape dialog box.

Figure 10.7 The Effects popup menu in the Brush Shape dialog box.

Magic Wand tool

The Magic Wand tool is used to select areas of the same color.

1. Click the Magic Wand tool in the Toolbox.

2. Click the color you want to select. All touching or adjacent pixels of this color are selected (see Figure 10.4).

To select more than one color, drag the Magic Wand tool across all of the colors you want to select.

Brush tool

The Brush tool is a freehand drawing tool that gives a paintbrush effect.

To use the Brush tool:

1. Click the Brush tool in the Toolbox.

2. Drag the Brush tool across the document wherever you want the paintbrush effect (see Figure 10.5).

Changing brush size and angle

You can change how large the brush is, what angle it is held at, or the intensity of the color applied.

To change Brush effects:

1. Double-click the Brush in the Toolbox. The Brush Shape dialog box appears (see Figure 10. 6).

2. Click the Brush shape or angle you want to use in the Brush Shape dialog box.

3. To change the intensity of the color, click the Effects popup menu in the Brush Shape dialog box and select one of the Effects choices: Normal, Blend, Lighter, Darker, or Tint (see Figure 10.7).

Pencil tool

The Pencil tool creates fine, sharp freehand-style lines, like drawing with a real pencil. The Pencil is also used to edit drawings pixel by pixel.

1. Click the Pencil tool in the Toolbox.

2. Drag the pencil using the mouse to create lines (see Figure 10.8).

Paint Bucket tool

The Paint Bucket is used to fill large areas with color. The areas must either be the background, or an enclosed image.

To use the Paint Bucket tool:

1. Select the color you want to use with the Paint Bucket from the Fill palette (see Figure 10.9).

2. Select the Paint Bucket from the Toolbox.

3. Click where you want the color to appear (see Figure 10.10).

Figure 10.8 Using the Pencil tool.

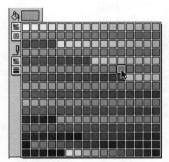

Figure 10.9 Selecting a color from the Fill palette.

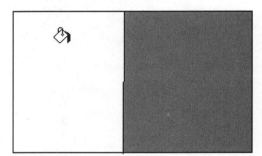

Figure 10.10 Using the Paint Bucket.

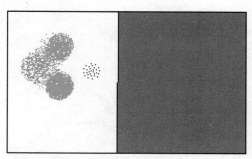

Figure 10.11 Using the Spray Can.

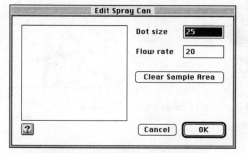

Figure 10.12 The Edit Spray Can dialog box.

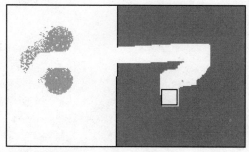

Figure 10.13 Using the Eraser.

Spray Can tool

The Spray Can tool gives a fine spray of color within the drawing.

To use the Spray Can tool:

1. Select the color you want to use from the Fill Palette.

2. Select the Spray Can from the Toolbox.

3. Click where you want the color to appear (see Figure 10.11).

Changing Spray Can attributes

You can change the dot size of the spray and how rapidly it flows from the Spray Can.

To change Spray Can attributes:

1. Double-click the Spray Can in the Toolbox. The Edit Spray Can dialog box appears (see Figure 10.12).

2. Change the Dot Size to make the spray dots larger or smaller in the Dots field.

3. Change the Flow Rate in the Flow Rate box to make more or fewer dots appear when the spray can is used.

4. Click the OK button when you are finished.

Eraser tool

The Eraser tool is used to erase parts of a drawing. It turns the erased areas white.

To use the Eraser tool:

1. Click the Eraser tool in the Toolbox.

2. Drag the Eraser tool over the areas of the drawing you want to erase. The areas turn to white (see Figure 10.13).

To erase the entire document, double-click the Eraser tool in the Toolbox.

SPRAY CAN TOOL

Creating a painting

Paintings may be created within the Painting module, or within other documents inside of a painting frame.

To create a Painting frame:

1. In any module of AppleWorks except Communications, click the Paint tool.

2. Click and drag a rectangle with the Paint tool to create a Painting frame in the document (see Figure 10.14).

3. Paint inside of the Painting frame (see Figure 10.15).

Once you have a frame created, when you click inside of the frame you have access to all Painting functions.

Figure 10.14 Creating a Painting frame with the Paint tool.

Figure 10.15 Painting inside the frame.

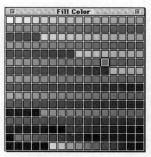

Figure 10.16 The Fill Color palette.

Figure 10.17 The Fill Pattern palette.

Figure 10.18 The Gradient palette.

Figure 10.19 The Fill Texture palette.

Figure 10.20 Selecting Pattern from the Options menu.

Color attributes

Color may be applied in the same way it was applied in Drawing. You may use:

- Color palettes (see Figure 10.16).
- Pattern palettes (see Figure 10.17).
- Gradient palettes (see Figure 10.18).
- Texture palettes (see Figure 10.19).

You have more control over color in Painting than in Drawing. You can change patterns, gradients, or textures.

Editing patterns

To change patterns:

1. Choose Patterns from the Options menu (see Figure 10. 20).

2. The Pattern Editor dialog box appears (see Figure 10.21). Click where you want a pixel to appear in the magnified version of the pattern.

3. Click the Invert button to change all of the blacks to white, and whites to black.

4. Click the OK button when you are finished.

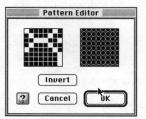

Figure 10.21 The Pattern Editor dialog box.

Editing textures

To change a texture:

1. Choose Textures from the Options menu. The Edit Texture dialog box appears (see Figure 10.22).

2. Click the Color popup box to select a color to use.

3. Click in the texture where you want to place the color.

4. Click the Revert button to change the texture back to the original pattern.

5. Click the Fill button to fill the entire texture with the current color.

Editing gradients

Gradients are fills with gradual changes of color. Gradients have a point of focus, such as the center, side, or top of the area to be filled. Both the colors of a gradient and the point of focus may be edited.

To edit a gradient:

1. Choose Gradients from the Options menu. The Gradient Editor dialog box appears (see Figure 10.23).

2. Select the Sweep popup menu.

3. Choose the style of sweep you want for the gradient.

4. Select one of the color buttons. The color palette appears.

5. Select the color you want to use with the gradient (see Figure 10.24).

6. Click the OK button when you are done.

You may change the type of sweep based on the three types: Directional, Circular, or Shape Burst.

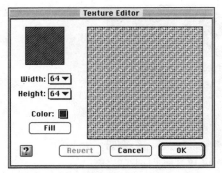

Figure 10.22 The Texture Editor dialog box.

Figure 10.23 Selecting Gradients from the Options menu.

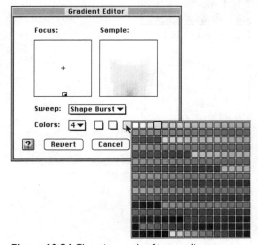

Figure 10.24 Choosing a color for a gradient.

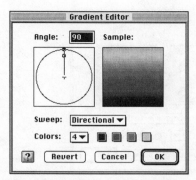

Figure 10.25 Directional gradient options.

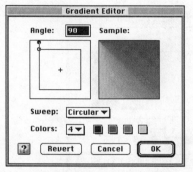

Figure 10.26 Circular gradient options.

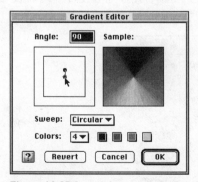

Figure 10.27 Setting the center of a Circular gradient.

Editing Directional Sweeps

1. Choose Gradient from the Options menu. The Edit Gradient dialog box appears.

2. Select the Sweep popup menu.

3. Choose Directional from the Sweep popup menu (see Figure 10.25).

4. Drag the sweep arm in the Angle pane of the Gradient Editor. The angle of the color gradient changes.

5. Click the OK button when you are finished.

Editing Circular Sweeps

1. Choose Gradient from the Options menu. The Edit Gradient dialog box appears.

2. Select the Sweep popup menu.

3. Choose Circular from the Sweep popup menu (see Figure 10.26).

4. Move the double-dot icon in the Angle pane (see Figure 10.27) so that the white dot appears where you want the center of the circular gradient to appear.

5. Rotate the black dot so that the gradient colors are rotated at the desired angle.

6. Click the OK button when you are finished.

EDITING GRADIENTS

Editing Shape Bursts

1. Choose Shape Burst from the Options menu. The Edit Gradient dialog box appears.

2. Select the Sweep popup menu.

3. Choose Shape Burst from the Sweep popup menu.

4. Drag the square button in the Focus pane of the Edit Gradient dialog box until the focus or center of the shape is appropriate (see Figure 10.28).

5. Select the number of colors to use in the Shape Burst from the Colors popup menu (see Figure 10.29).

6. Click the OK button when you are finished.

Editing pixels

Pixels are the basic elements of a painting. They appear on screen as square dots. You can change how close you zoom to the painting in order to see and edit each pixel.

To edit pixels:

1. Click the Zoom Out or the Zoom In box at the bottom of the window (see Figure 10.30)

2. Choose the Pencil tool from the Toolbox.

3. Click the color you want to use in the Fill Color palette.

4. Click the pixel you want to change in the drawing (see Figure 10.31).

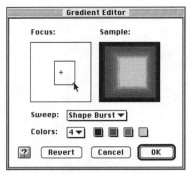

Figure 10.28 Adjusting the focus of a Shape Burst gradient.

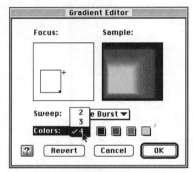

Figure 10.29 Setting the number of colors for a Shape Burst gradient.

Figure 10.30 The Zoom bar.

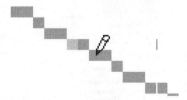

Figure 10.31 Editing individual pixels.

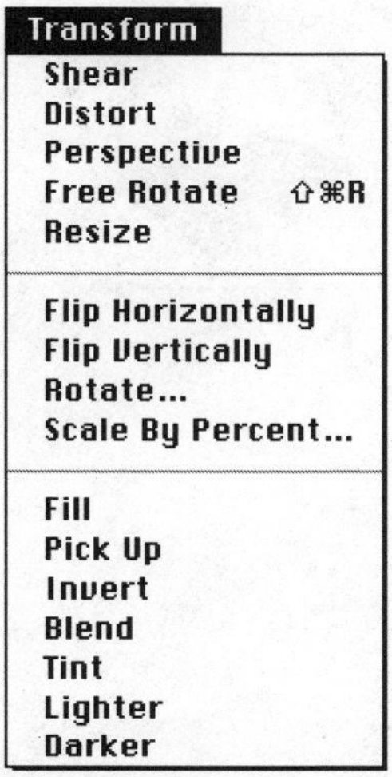

```
┌─────────────────────────┐
│ Transform               │
│ Shear                   │
│ Distort                 │
│ Perspective             │
│ Free Rotate      ⇧⌘R   │
│ Resize                  │
│                         │
│ Flip Horizontally       │
│ Flip Vertically         │
│ Rotate...               │
│ Scale By Percent...     │
│                         │
│ Fill                    │
│ Pick Up                 │
│ Invert                  │
│ Blend                   │
│ Tint                    │
│ Lighter                 │
│ Darker                  │
└─────────────────────────┘
```

Figure 10.32 The Transform menu.

Tinting, blending, and reversing colors

You may change colors by filling an image with a new color, tinting a color either a lighter or darker shade, blending two colors together, or reversing a color.

1. Select the Rectangle Selection tool from the Toolbox.

2. Drag the Selection tool around the area you want to change.

3. Choose one of the following options (see Figure 10.32).

—To reverse a color select Invert from the Transform menu.

—To blend a color select Blend from the Transform menu.

—To tint a color select Tint from the Transform menu.

—To make a color lighter, select Lighter from the Transform menu.

—To make a color darker, select Darker from the Transform menu.

Transforming an image

Transforming in image means changing its shape or orientation. When you Transform an image you may Shear, Distort, Resize, Rotate, or add Perspective to a selection.

Shear

To Shear an image:

1. Select the Rectangle Selection tool from the toolbox.

2. Surround the area of the image you want to reshape.

3. Select Shear from the Transform menu. The surrounding selection appears with a dot on each corner.

4. Click the upper right corner of the rectangular selection.

5. Drag the rectangle into the appropriate angle (see Figure 10.33).

Distort or add perspective

To distort or add perspective:

1. Select the Rectangle Selection tool from the toolbox.

2. Surround the area of the image you want to reshape.

3. Select Distort or Perspective from the Transform menu. The surrounding selection appears with a dot on each corner.

4. Click the upper right corner of the rectangular selection.

5. Drag the rectangle into the appropriate angle (see Figure 10.34 and 10.35).

Figure 10.33 Shearing an image.

Figure 10.34 Distorting an image.

Figure 10.35 Adding perspective to an image.

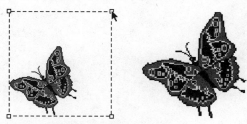

Figure 10.36 Resizing an image.

Resizing an image

1. Select the Rectangle Selection tool from the toolbox.

2. Surround the area of the image you want to resize.

3. Select Resize from the Transform menu. The surrounding selection appears with a dot on each corner.

4. Click the upper right corner of the rectangular selection.

5. Drag the rectangle into the appropriate size (see Figure 10.36).

TRANSFORMING AN IMAGE

COMMUNICATIONS

Figure 11.1 Creating a name and an icon for the session is the first step to connecting with any type of service.

Figure 11.2 Fill out the phone number and modem type.

AppleWorks Communications can send Fax documents and Email, log or capture sessions, and connect to your ISP (Internet Service Provider). You can also connect to BBSs (Bulletin Board Services). The world of the Internet is fully open to you, and making connections is as easy as 1-2-3.

The basic communications steps include:

1. Choose a name for the connection you want to make (see Figure 11.1).

2. Fill out the telephone number and modem type in the Phone Number dialog box (see Figure 11.2).

3. Dial the number.

With these simple steps you can connect to the world of cyberspace within just a few minutes.

To send faxes using AppleWorks you need a *fax modem*—a modem that is capable of sending and receiving faxes from a fax machine or computer.

Communications for Windows 95

The instructions for setting up communications for Macintosh are different from the instructions for Windows 95. If you're using AppleWorks on a Macintosh, skip ahead to "Communications for the Macintosh" later in this chapter.

To start your first connection:

1. Select New from the File menu in the Communications module. The Communications wizard appears (see Figure 11.3).

2. Type a name in the Name box of the New Communications dialog box.

3. Choose an icon from the icon list that is appropriate for this new connection.

4. Click the OK button. The Phone Number dialog box appears (see Figure 11.4).

5. Make any corrections that need to be made in the Phone Number dialog box to the information that AppleWorks fills out for you in the Phone Number dialog box, such as the country you are calling from, your area code, or your modem type.

6. Type the phone number for the ISP. You may type the phone number without dashes, for example: *7777777*.

7. Click the OK button when you are finished. The Connect dialog box appears (see Figure 11.5).

8. Click the Dial button. The modem should begin dialing immediately.

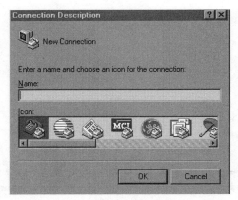

Figure 11.3 Many of the icons are set up to represent commercial ISPs (Internet Service Providers).

Figure 11.4 The Phone Number dialog box.

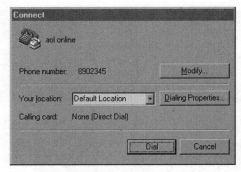

Figure 11.5 The Connect dialog box.

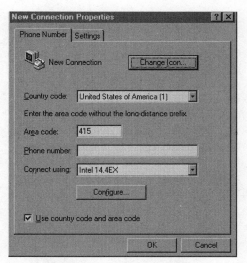

Figure 11.6 The Phone Connection Properties dialog box.

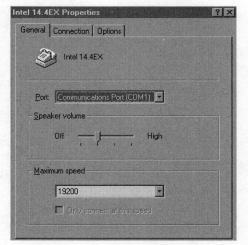

Figure 11.7 The Modem Properties dialog box.

Setting up your terminal

To set up a terminal:

When you use the Communications wizards, it is possible the modem type doesn't match what you have as a modem. AppleWorks is designed to detect the modem and where it is connected, which is usually Com port 1 (communications port 1). This part of the program is almost always correct, but in case it isn't, here is what you do:

1. Select Properties from the File menu. The New Connection Properties dialog box appears (see Figure 11.6).

2. Click the Phone Number tab in the Properties dialog box.

3. Make any changes to the country, area code, or telephone number in the Properties dialog box.

4. To change the modem, click the modem pop-up menu and select the appropriate modem.

5. Click the Configure button at the bottom of the New Connection Properties dialog box. The Modem Properties dialog box appears (see Figure 11.7).

6. Click the Port pop-up menu and change the connection information for the modem if it is incorrect.

7. Slide the Speaker Volume slider to raise or lower the volume from the modem speaker.

8. Click the Maximum Speed pop-up menu and select the proper modem speed.

9. Click the OK button when you are done.

SETTING UP YOUR TERMINAL

Changing connection settings

Connection settings are settings that make sure the modem and the ISP are compatible. They include:

- Data bits
- Parity
- Stop bits
- Error control
- Flow control

These advanced settings usually do not need to be changed, but you may need to change them in order to connect to a specific ISP or BBS.

To change connection settings:

1. Select Properties from the File box. The Properties dialog box appears.

2. Click the Configure button at the bottom of the Properties dialog box. The New Connection Properties box appears.

3. Click the Connection tab at the top of the Properties dialog box. The Connections panel appears.

4. Change the Data bits, parity, or stop bits as required by the ISP or BBS to which you are connecting.

5. Select the proper Call preferences in the call preferences pane.

6. Click the Port button at the bottom of the Properties dialog box to make advanced port settings to the buffers required by the party to which you are connecting.

7. Click the OK button when you are done.

✔ Tip

- If someone has made changes in this box, and the changes are not working for the connection you are trying to make, click the Default button to return the settings to the standard settings for the modem type previously selected.

Listen for the Squeal

One way to tell when the modem is about to connect to an ISP is to listen for the squeal the modem makes when it recognizes the ISP. Once the squeal is silent, the modem and ISP are usually connected. If you have an external modem, the light that is labeled OH or off hook should be lit up. Off hook means the telephone is ready to dial, as you are when you take the telephone receiver off the hook.

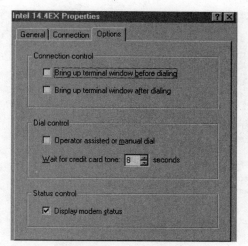

Figure 11.8 The Modem Properties Options panel. Select "Operator assisted or manual dial" when dialing through a Centrex system such as the systems found at most major hotels.

Miscellaneous modem settings

Several advanced settings can make the modem work more efficiently, including settings for displaying connection information and settings to pause the modem.

To change these settings:

1. Select Properties from the File menu. The Properties dialog box appears.

2. Click the Configure button at the bottom of the Properties dialog box. The Modem Properties dialog box appears (see Figure 11.8).

3. Click the Options tab in the New Connection Settings dialog box. The Options panel appears.

4. Select any of the options you want to change, including:

   —Bring up terminal window before or after dialing

   —Operator assisted or manual dialing

   —Display modem status

5. Click the OK button when you are done.

Saving and Retrieving previous settings

Once the Session is set up and all of the properties are correct, the connection and dialing settings may be saved by selecting Save from the File menu and giving the communication settings a name, just as you would give a name to a word processing document.

To retrieve settings:

1. Choose Open from the File menu. The Open dialog box appears (see Figure 11.9).

2. Select the appropriate settings from the Open dialog box.

3. To dial the number, select Connect from the Call menu.

To hang up, select Disconnect from the Call menu.

Transferring information

Transferring information to and from an ISP can be done several ways:

■ Include information in an E-mail as part of an E-mail message

■ Attach a file to an E-mail message and send it

■ Upload a file by choosing Send File from the Transfer menu

■ Download a file by choosing Receive File from the Transfer menu

Download means to transfer a file from an ISP to your home computer without using an Email message; downloading is the cyberspace version of copy. Upload means to transfer a file from your home computer to the ISP.

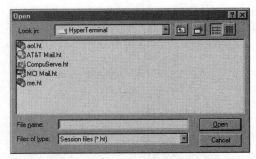

Figure 11.9 The icons in the Open dialog box are the icons that were selected in the New Communications setup from the File menu.

SAVING SETTINGS

Figure 11.10 The Send Text File dialog box. Text files transfer the fastest of all files because they contain no formatting.

Communication Tips

When you send a file to another party, it's best if they have the same program that you have, and the same version of the program. For example, if you send an MS Word version 6.0 file to someone who does not have MS Word, they won't be able to read the file.

Likewise, if you send a WordPerfect version 8 to someone who only has WordPerfect version 6, they will not be able to read the file. This is called backward incompatibility. Backward incompatibility means that older versions of a program cannot use files created in newer versions of the program.

Sending a file or document

This version of AppleWorks Communications makes it easier than ever to send files.

To send a file:

1. Select Send File from the Transfer menu. The Send File dialog box appears.

2. Click the Browse button in the Send File dialog box. The File dialog box appears.

3. Select the file you want to send from the File dialog box.

4. Click the Open button. The Send File dialog box reappears.

5. Select the Protocol to send the file from the Protocol pop-up menu.

6. Click the send button when you are done and ready to send the file.

✔ Tip

■ Zmodem is the most common protocol, so if you do not know what to select, use Zmodem protocol.

Sending a text file

"Text" files are quicker to send than regular document files. A text file is a file with only words and numbers and no formatting.

To send a text file:

1. Select Send Text File from the Transfer menu. The Send Text File dialog box appears. (see Figure 11.10).

2. Select the text file you want to send from the dialog box.

3. Click the Open button. The text file is immediately sent.

SENDING FILES

Receiving a file

Receiving a file is almost the same as sending one.

To receive a file:

1. Make sure you are connected to the other party. If you have an external modem, you can make sure you are connected by noticing that the OH light is on and the RD light is flickering.

2. Choose Receive File from the Transfer menu. The Receive File dialog box appears (see Figure 11.11).

3. Select the Browse button next to the "Place received file..." field.

4. Find where you want the file to be placed when it is downloaded.

5. Click the OK button. The Receive File dialog box appears.

6. Select the Protocol to send the file from the Protocol pop-up menu.

7. Click the Receive button when you are ready to receive the file. If you have an external modem, the RD light on the modem will blink vigorously, indicating that the modem is receiving the file.

✔ Tip

■ Just as in sending files, Zmodem is the most common protocol, but in the case of receiving files, your protocol must be the same as the party that is sending the file. If they send the file using Zmodem, you must receive the file using Zmodem; but if they send the file using Ymodem, you must change your protocol to Y modem.

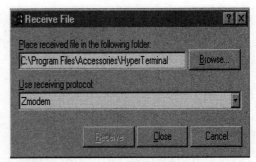

Figure 11.11 The Receive File dialog box.

Figure 11.12 Command line interfaces, like the Unix interface above, are easily recorded using Capture.

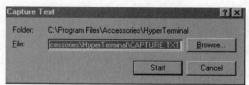

Figure 11.13 The Capture Text dialog box.

Capturing a session

A session refers to the period that you are online. To "capture" a session means to record everything that goes on while you are online. Another way of referring to capturing a session is to say that you are "logging" a session. Logs or captures are used when you need to keep the information and commands that you use while you are on the computer (see Figure 11.12).

Captures and logs do not work from AppleWorks while you are on an ISP such as America Online. AOL has its own method of logging sessions. Capture only records text information. Text information is what you see when you use "command line" interfaces rather than GUI (graphic user interfaces) programs such as America Online.

To capture a session:

1. Select Capture Text from the Transfer menu. The Capture Text dialog box appears (see Figure 11.13).

2. Select the Browse button by the Place Received file field in the Receive File dialog box.

3. Find where you want the file to be placed when it is downloaded.

4. Give the File a name in the Name box.

5. Click the OK button when you are finished. The Capture Text dialog box reappears.

6. Click the Start button when you are ready to start capturing a session.

Capturing a session to the printer

Capture a session to the printer records all actions you take and immediately prints them out. To capture a session to the printer select Capture to Printer from the Transfer menu.

Paste to Host

Copy and Paste may be used with
Communications just as they may be used
with any of the AppleWorks Modules.

To paste using Communications:

1. Copy the information you want to paste.
   For example: you may want to type the
   text for your web page in AppleWorks
   word processing and copy the text to the
   computer that is going to host your files.

2. Dial the computer to which you want to
   connect.

3. Open the program that you want to use
   on the computer you just dialed. For
   example: Pico is a simple text editor on a
   Unix system. If you want to use Pico to
   finish a web page, you must start Pico and
   open a blank page.

4. Click the place in the receiving machine
   where you want the information to be
   pasted.

5. Select Paste to Host from the Edit menu.
   The text is pasted (see Figure 11.14).

Sending Email

AppleWorks Communications is not an Email
program. You will need Claris Emailer,
Eudora, Netscape, Internet Explorer, or any
other Email program to send mail once
Communications has connected you to
another machine.

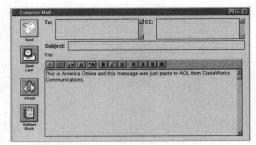

Figure 11.14 Using Paste to Host.

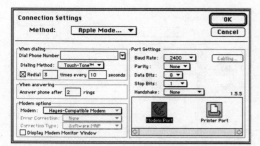

Figure 11.15 The Connections Settings dialog box for Macintosh.

Communications for the Macintosh

The instructions for Communications for the Macintosh are different from the instructions for Windows 95. If you are using AppleWorks on Windows 95, see "Communications for Windows 95" earlier in this chapter.

To start communications on the Macintosh:

1. Select Communications from the Settings menu. The Communication dialog box appears (see Figure 11.15).

2. Select the communications method from the Method pop-up menu. Usually you will use Apple Modem Tool.

3. Type the phone number you want to dial in the Dial Phone Number box.

4. Select the appropriate dialing method (either Touch Tone or Pulse) from the Dialing Method pop-up menu.

5. Select the appropriate port settings in the Port Settings area of the communication dialog box. This includes modem speed (baud rate), Parity, Data bits, and Stop bits.

6. Click the OK button when you are finished.

COMMUNICATIONS FOR THE MACINTOSH

Terminal Settings

Once you have made the correct Communications settings, you need to make correct Terminal settings.

To make Terminal settings:

1. Select Terminal from the Settings menu. The Terminal Settings dialog box appears (see Figure 11.16).

2. Select the appropriate Emulation from the Emulation pop-up menu. The usual emulation is VT102.

3. Click the OK button when you are finished.

Dialing a number

To dial a number, select Open Connection from the Session menu, or press Shift-⌘-O (see Figure 11.17).

Transferring Information

Transferring information is done from both the Transfer menu and Session menu.

To transfer information:

1. Select Transfer from the Settings menu. The File Transfer Settings dialog box appears (see Figure 11.18).

2. Select the proper protocol from the Protocol pop-up menu. The protocol should match that of the sending or receiving party.

3. Click the OK button when you are finished.

4. Select Send File from the Session menu. The Send File dialog box appears (see Figure 11.19).

5. Select the file to send and press the OK button.

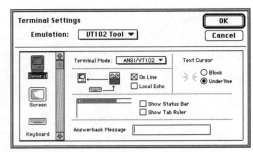

Figure 11.16 The Terminal Settings dialog box.

Figure 11.17 Choosing Open Connection.

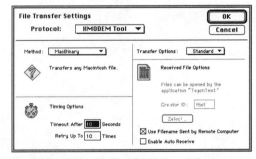

Figure 11.18 The File Transfer Settings dialog box.

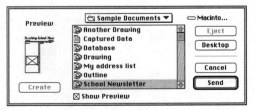

Figure 11.19 The Send File dialog box.

TERMINAL SETTINGS

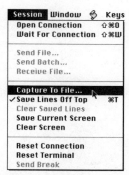

Figure 11.20 Choosing Capture To File from the Session menu.

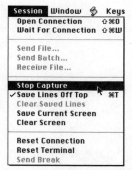

Figure 11.21 "Capture To File" changes to "Stop Capture" once the capturing process begins.

Capturing a session

To capture a session:

1. Select Capture To File from the Session menu (see Figure 11.20). The Save File dialog box appears.

2. Type a name for the captured session in the Save File dialog box.

3. Click the OK button. The capture session begins.

Stopping a capture

Stopping a capture is the reverse of starting a capture. Select Stop Capture from the Session menu (see Figure 11.21). Stop Capture appears where Capture to File appears in the Session menu once the session capturing is started.

INDEX

INDEX

INDEX